T0054618

Pots, Techniques, and Projects to Transform Any Space

CONTAINER GARDENER'S HANDBOOK

FRANCES TOPHILL

Photography by Rachel Warne

Container Gardener's Handbook

CompanionHouse Books™ is an imprint of Fox Chapel Publishers International Ltd.

CompanionHouse Books Project Team
Vice President-Content: Christopher Reggio
Editor: Amy Deputato
Art Director: Mary Ann Kahn

First published in Great Britain in 2017 by
Kyle Books, an imprint of Kyle Cathie Limited
192–198 Vauxhall Bridge Road
London SW1V 1DX
www.kylebooks.co.uk

Text © Frances Tophill 2017
Photographs © Rachel Warne 2017
Design © Kyle Books 2017
Editor: Vicky Orchard
Design: Helen Bratby
Photography: Rachel Warne
Production: Lisa Pinnell

All rights reserved. No part of this book may be reproduced, stored in a retrieval system, or transmitted in any form or by any means, electronic, mechanical, photocopying, recording, or otherwise, without the prior written permission of Fox Chapel Publishers, except for the inclusion of brief quotations in an acknowledged review.

ISBN 978-1-62008-330-7

Library of Congress Cataloging-in-Publication Data

Names: Tophill, Frances, author.
Title: Container gardener's handbook : pots, techniques, and projects to
   transform any space / Frances Tophill.
Description: Mount Joy, PA : Fox Chapel Publishing, [2019] | Includes index.
   Identifiers: LCCN 2018043589 (print) | LCCN 2018047019 (ebook) | ISBN
   9781620083314 (ebook) | ISBN 9781620083307 (softcover)
Subjects: LCSH: Container gardening.
Classification: LCC SB418 (ebook) | LCC SB418 .T67 2019 (print) | DDC
   635.9/86--dc23
LC record available at https://lccn.loc.gov/2018043589

This book has been published with the intent to provide accurate and authoritative information in regard to the subject matter within. While every precaution has been taken in the preparation of this book, the author and publisher expressly disclaim any responsibility for any errors, omissions, or adverse effects arising from the use or application of the information contained herein.

Fox Chapel Publishing
903 Square Street
Mount Joy, PA 17552

Fox Chapel Publishers International Ltd.
7 Danefield Road, Selsey (Chichester)
West Sussex PO20 9DA, U.K.

www.facebook.com/companionhousebooks

We are always looking for talented authors. To submit an idea, please send a brief inquiry to acquisitions@foxchapelpublishing.com

Printed and bound in China
22 21 20 19   2 4 6 8 10 9 7 5 3 1

WHY SHOULD WE GARDEN WITH CONTAINERS?

I can think of four great reasons:

1. The first is that containers are so convenient. No matter how much or, crucially, how little space you have, containers help us to bring greenery, scents, colors, and edibles into our lives.

2. Containers also offer you flexibility in your garden design because you can move pots around or change their contents. This is a great asset; growing conditions that would otherwise be inherently unchanging can be exploited to their full potential. If a plant isn't happy where it is, you can move it—with no disruption—from shade to sunshine or from a windy spot to a sheltered nook. The ability to move a plant is really useful and means you can grow many plants that otherwise might not thrive in your plot.

3. Another obvious benefit is that pots contain the roots of a plant, which is useful for a number of reasons. It might be necessary to prevent a plant from spreading, such as with a bonsai tree or a very vigorous bamboo, or a plant may need special conditions, such as a very specific soil type that is not present in your garden, extra drainage, or a particularly acidic environment (see pages 9 and 136). It also helps to hold roots in a space that is usually inhospitable, giving them the opportunity to feed and hold on against the odds—such as on a wall or windowsill.

4. Believe it or not, pots have fantastic design potential. With so many different shapes, sizes, and colors of containers and a whole kingdom of plants to play with, they can add a brilliant and varying aesthetic to your garden. Close your eyes and imagine a planted pot. I bet I can guess the first thing that popped into your head: the pot was terra-cotta and had something flowery in it. A *geranium*, let's say. Or maybe it was a hanging basket? Perhaps something with petunias trailing over the sides? The point I am trying to make is that, for some, growing in containers has become something of a clichéd concept. We tend to think of fail-safe, tried-and-true arrangements. However, there is so much choice and with the further options of upcycling—and even of making your own pots—there really is no excuse for thinking that there's only one way of growing in containers. Think outside the box (or should I say pot?) and try something different.

Plants are good for the soul; they purify the air around us and fill our spaces with pockets of green (one of the most soothing colors) as well as providing havens for wildlife. Plants are also useful: we eat them, we put them in vases, we make dye with them, and we use them as the basis for all kinds of medicine. So whatever your space, there really is no excuse for not making a little room for a plant or two. Even just a couple of plants will give you joy and a sense of tranquility as you nurture them and watch them grow. What better activity is there to do with your children or friends or for some peaceful creative time than fashioning a container that will be exactly what you want, filled with plants you love?

There is a knack to achieving the perfect container. I've seen some done badly or packed with insufficient or dull bedding. People tend to revert to the fail-safe option of alternating bulbs in the spring with bedding plants in the summer and then maybe some pansies in the winter, if they can be bothered. These types of displays, the kind commonly planted by clubs or in public parks, are uninspiring, to say the least. But containers need not be synonymous with these kinds of safe and predictable displays. These poor pots, brimming with potential, didn't ask to be filled with the same old species, without color or form even being a consideration. All that compost, all those nutrients, could have gone to feed and nurture something truly exquisite. There is a whole world of potential to be unlocked from containers that are just sitting in the shed or around the side of the house collecting dust, weeds, moss, and possibly spiders. I implore you to resurrect, revamp, and replant these containers and, this time around, give them a chance to shine. Think of them as the key element of your design, not just a finishing touch or an afterthought. Unleash their true potential.

Succulents from the genus *Crassula* or *Haworthia* bring beauty to a small corner of a greenhouse.

Fuchsia and hardy Geranium add flair to a pot display using easily available species.

That's what sets growing in containers apart from all other kinds of horticulture, but there is a whole host of other reasons why you should choose growing in containers over traditional flower beds.

Cost is one; increasingly when we spend money on our gardens, we tend to see gardening as less important and invest in furnishings and hard landscaping rather than plants. Plants can be surprisingly expensive, and, if they are transplantd, they generally can't be taken with us when we move—not without some considerable effort and advance planning, and some may not survive the disruption. Growing your favorite specimens in containers is a cost-effective way of filling your outdoor space while still incorporating some greenery, and you can take the plants with you if you move. If you have a good-sized space to fill, containers have another clever cost-cutting advantage—because the container adds bulk to the garden, it reduces the need for so many plants to fill the space and stands in for costly hard landscaping.

Ease is also an important plus for containers. Growing plants in a container is easy. You don't have to do any soil analysis before choosing your plants—you can just choose something you like and stick it in the pot with some multipurpose compost, and it will usually grow with relative success. Even trees will be happy in pots for years with some feeding and a little water.

Don't confuse ease of planting with being low maintenance. A container plant is reliant on you for survival. In the ground, nature throws all sorts of things at a plant, but if it survives these trials and tribulations, chances are, once it's established, nature will also nurture it. The rain will water it, the leaves falling on the ground will provide it with nutrients and the unconfined earth will give the roots plenty of room to grow. In a container, this is not the case; resources are finite and hard to come by. The designing and the planting process may be easy, but be prepared that maintenance can be considerably more intensive.

By carefully choosing plants that are happy in containers, you give yourself less work and less worry. Maintaining plants in pots isn't as onerous as double-digging your vegetable plot or pulling weeds from your flower beds, but they need a careful eye and an occasional water and feed, and they may need bigger containers when they get too big for their pots (every few years).

You can also grow something in a pot that you might not be able to grow in a flower bed. Some plants need specific soils, light levels, or temperatures that your garden cannot provide; when it comes to your garden, there is very little you can do to alter the conditions. Hence the often-repeated phrase "right plant, right place." However, when it comes to containers, that rule goes merrily out the window. You can choose the conditions you want: use an acidic compost for an acid-loving plant,
add lime for plants that prefer alkaline conditions, position the pot in a sunny spot if the plant needs heat. Dig in some gravel to add drainage and compost to help it retain more nutrients, and even move it indoors when it gets too cold. Being able to nurture a plant in a very specific environment is extremely handy and can be essential to growing that plant well.

I love container growing because of my lack of outdoor space—the good ground I have to grow in is incredibly limited. I am very lucky to have a small balcony when many of us don't even have that. A patio may be the extent of your "land'" or perhaps just a porch, windowsill, doorstep, or even (if you're very lucky) a roof terrace. For the many of us facing this problem, container growing is the ideal solution. Pots fill my windowsills, tables, ledges, desk, doorstep, and, quite frankly, anywhere I can shoe-horn

them in. Containers can fit into any space; they can hang from the ceiling, climb the walls, sit on shelves, and be incorporated into even the smallest spaces, making them versatile, to say the least.

And, finally, those who are lucky enough not to struggle with space are in the wonderful position of being able to have some massive containers if they so desire. That doesn't just mean big pots; raised beds are a form of large container, as are walls with growing space at the top, huge urns, installations of every shape, and designs made of any material you can imagine.

Alpine plants bring greenery with inobtrusive foliage and often delicate and beautiful flowers to almost any area, as long as it gets enough light.

Aeoniums of different colors and sizes make a dramatic and architectural centerpiece to an otherwise fairly traditional potted-plant display.

Containers are also invaluable in terms of both plant and garden design. The variety of shapes, sizes, styles, and materials, combined with the ways in which you can arrange them, where you position them, how you plant around them, how many pots you use, and whether you stick to one color for a sleek, minimalist finish or mix and match them in a shabby-chic, bohemian way, creates almost endless opportunities for dynamic designs. Add to this the huge choice of plants available, and you have a world of options to choose from.

For the more traditional, try terra-cotta pots filled with bedding plants that are changed in the spring and autumn to give year-round color. Or you can use cushion mosses underneath a single-colored plant for impact and an uncomplicated design. Move up the evolutionary timeline toward ferns; try horsetails with striking verticals or the delicate fronds of an asparagus fern for cloud-like texture. You can even do away with the soil altogether and fill containers with water for a hydroponic system or to create an indoor pond. If you have walls or stony ground without much soil, you can grow succulents or alpines with shallow root systems to fill every nook and cranny, or you can grow tropical plants in a damp, warm area with rich soil.

There's no end to the combinations you can create with just a little inspiration, but if that seems a little daunting, I'm here to help. In this book, I'll show you a wide range of ideas for all tastes to get you growing—but don't forget to do it your way. Grow the plants you like in your favorite pots so that they give you results that are personal, beautiful, innovative, rewarding, and productive in a style that reflects you and your home.

If you've dismissed gardening as something that seems beyond you or your space, it's time to think again. With just a little thought and planning, container gardening can fit into a modern way of life and can be a lot more varied and exciting than you might expect. So let's get started!

An arid, urban area with poor soil that lends itself to Mediterranean species like olive and thyme is hugely enhanced by some modern herb garden containers for marjoram, hyssop and lavender.

THE POTS

Technically, a flowerpot is just something that holds the growing medium and the plants. It doesn't have to be a set shape or size or material. It can be something repurposed, something homemade, or something you might never even think of as a container. With so much choice, it helps to know your options and which pots best lend themselves to which plants. Armed with the right information, your pot displays can really have the edge.

CHOOSING THE RIGHT SIZE

Generally, containers sit on the ground or on a hard surface, but don't forget that there is also the option of using wall-mounted or hanging pots. Wherever you put your containers, when choosing your pots, you need to think carefully about what you will use in relation to where they will be situated.

The keys to choosing the right container for a specific place are its weight and size. For a container that sits on the ground in a permanent position, there are more options, simply because the combined weight of the pot and the soil is not an issue. On the ground, you can create small, dainty arrangements with several little pots gathered together, or you can use huge raised beds, troughs, urns, or any other really large containers.

If you want to put your container on the floor of a balcony or roof terrace, you need to weigh the options more carefully. A fully finished and watered container is not a lightweight feature—the water alone can weigh a lot (1 liter weighs 2.2 pounds [1 kg]), and when it is added to a heavy pot filled with soil...you get the picture. The last thing you want to do is overburden your balcony or roof terrace with weighty items; this can be very dangerous if the area can't take the load. However, one way of getting around this is by reducing the amount of heavy soil in a container and bulking it up with lightweight polystyrene or something similar. Don't use too much—just enough to make the containers a little less hefty. If you are thinking about a shelf or other wall-mounted system, keep in mind that you will need even lighter loads and smaller pots.

BIG CONTAINERS

Containers come in all shapes and sizes. I have two large containers in my front yard in the form of raised beds. This is partly because I cannot grow much in the soil as it is mainly sand, and, because I live near the sea, it has a very high salt content. It also doesn't drain very well (unusual for a sandy soil—lucky me!), so I had no choice but to make two giant containers and fill them with better soil in which I actually have a chance of growing healthy plants.

Many gardeners face the same problems. It could be for all sorts of reasons—maybe you have unstable ground, inhospitable ground, trouble bending down to work at a low level, a solid concrete patio that you don't want to break up, or a problem with damp soil, or maybe you just like the look of raised beds as opposed to borders dug into the ground. You can get around these issues by building a container to fit your space and serve your needs, and it can be as big as you like or as big as looks right in your space. It can also have the bonus of doubling as a seat or storage with a bit of creative design.

An upcycled metal container makes a bold, modern feature, creating an innovative boundary. When softened with a planting scheme of *Eupatorium* and grasses, it looks more rustic.

But for those who do not enjoy building, there are all kinds of large containers available. They can be purpose-built containers (urns being a classic example) or something more contemporary, made of modern materials like concrete or rusted steel. They can also be something not originally intended to house plants but cleverly repurposed to do just that. I have even heard of cars being turned into huge containers with plants spilling out of the trunks, hoods, and windows. If you have the space, and you love to grow, then a large container does the best job of simulating the ground because it allows plenty of root space and nutrients. You can either grow a lot more of the plants you love or fewer mature, large specimens. A big container also makes a bold statement—something that, if you have the courage, can be the foundation of an outdoor space, even a small one.

Single species make a bold statement. This huge pot is planted with one of the biggest herbaceous perennials: *Gunnera macrophylla*.

A collection of simple, small pots is a very effective way of filling a pint-sized patch. By using all kinds of varying textures, you can create something eclectic, subtle, and undeniably beautiful, belying your space's diminutive beginnings.

SMALL CONTAINERS

If you only have limited space, don't despair—there is a vast array of containers you can use, as small as you like. There are all sorts of weird and wonderful ideas out there for making containers out of almost any material. The key consideration when using really small containers is the planting because you need to choose species that can cope with having their roots very restricted. The soil in a small container also tends to dry out and lose its nutrients quicker than that in a large pot. So unless you have a lot of time and love to give your containers, it's worth choosing fairly low-maintenance plants that can cope with dry, nutrient-poor, small spaces, or plants that are extremely slow growing. Plants such as *geraniums*, sedums, and other succulents; *Erigeron* and other wild daisies, and even many herbs such as lavender, thyme, and rosemary can cope with slightly drier, nutrient-poor conditions and, dare I say, neglect from us growers!

As a rule (and a hard-and-fast one at that), a plant whose roots are restricted will grow slowly. Generally, in containers and in the ground, what's going on above the soil directly correlates with what's going on below. So when the roots are unable to spread and grow, the stems and leaves will be likewise reduced. This is how the Japanese tradition of bonsai works; when the roots of a tree that would ordinarily be several stories tall has its growth restricted, the trunk, branches, and leaves are much smaller than they would be in the wild. Be warned that these trees do still need nutrients and a fair amount of water and thus are pretty high maintenance. However, for those with the time to dedicate to their bonsai (and my dad is someone who puts his all into his collection), a tree can be lovingly nurtured to grow for hundreds of years in one small pot and never grow taller than a few feet (see page 123).

This array of succulent plants in various small containers proves that there are no limits to the choices available to you with clever use of plants. Don't feel limited by these resilient plant species: their shapes and colors can be as varied as the receptacles in which they're planted.

CHOOSING THE RIGHT SHAPE

It is an old debate among gardeners: a square hole or a round one? I don't think it makes an enormous difference but, in a pot, this question has much bigger ramifications in terms of design rather than plant health. And the options are not just round or square but oblong, cylindrical, hexagonal, octagonal, triangular, short and wide, long and thin... The choice is yours, but it pays to think about it in advance if you want a cohesive design.

ROUND

Most containers tend to be round (for example, urns), but they can be subtly varied in shape, perhaps cylindrical or bowl-shaped. If you want to change things up, here are a few ideas on how to maximize the impact of round containers.

- Round containers look particularly good when displayed en masse. Round pots are some of the easiest to arrange in large displays and lend themselves to being positioned in corners or in circles.

- Place a large round pot at the center of a circular piece of concrete or deck or slightly off-center in a circular feature in your yard or garden.

- Arrange a few pots in a spiral or sprawling cluster; they look particularly nice if you use pots of varying sizes, with the largest positioned at the back.

- Generally, circular pots give a slightly rustic look, so they work well in a cottage-garden-style design or something a little more traditional, unless they are cylindrical or columnar, in which case they can create a striking statement.

It is hard to make square pots look haphazard, and they can be untidy-looking unless they are lined up perfectly, either in a diamond formation, as a bigger square, or in a straight line. For this reason, it can also be hard to combine square and round pots in the same space.

SQUARE

For a more modern-looking design, use square containers. To show them off at their best, try one of these ideas.

- Make them a stand-alone feature in your garden.

- They can be fantastic when placed alongside other square pots, either with a little separation between each container, such as four or five spaced evenly along a wall, or positioned right up against each other to make a continuous line of containers, which also can be used to create a boundary or pathway.

- Complement their modern look by using architectural plants in a simple planting scheme.

- Use them in a highly formal garden or something with an Italianate twist. They look equally good in an incredibly simple design, such as a Scandinavian or minimalist look.

TROUGH

This shape is a common type of floor planter and also frequently used on walls and windowsills. Troughs look good and also serve as raised beds of sorts, housing many plants and maximizing productivity. Here are a few ideas to make simple look sensational!

- Troughs make wonderful temporary or movable hedges, planted either with shrubs or less traditional hedging plants. Try using grasses, such as Miscanthus giganteus, or even sweet corn as a see-through hedge.

- Troughs are fantastic along a boundary or border to define the edges, or they can work as screens along the edges of windows or balconies or to hide unsightly parts of the yard, such as a compost area or shed.

- A small, narrow trough is a great option for a windowsill if you have limited space.

- As well as being placed on the ground, troughs can sit on any other hard surface, such as the top of a wall, if properly secured.

- Brighten up the bottom of a boring wall with colorfully planted troughs.

- Use troughs to create pathway edges in the yard or to separate certain areas of the garden.

- Use troughs not in a neat line, but staggered for dramatic effect, especially if planted with something tall and architectural.

RAISED BEDS

Raised beds are a step up from troughs and can be made to any height, which can make plant maintenance easier, particularly if you have problems with mobility. These large-scale containers are built up on the ground into any shape from any material you have on hand and can be as complicated or as simple as you like. They are versatile and can fit in with any designs, from the most rustic to the most contemporary.

- If you like the rustic look, raised beds can be created by building dry stone walls with large stones carefully piled together and cramming it with cottage-garden flowers tumbling over one another, perhaps even growing through the gaps in between the stones. Plants like Erigeron lend themselves beautifully to this look. You could give this an even more authentic English-garden feel by growing edibles or perhaps some herbs among the flowers. Leave an antique fork sticking out of the soil (for effect, of course—you should never leave your real tools out in all weather!), and you have a stunning traditional cottage-garden bed, all within a beautiful hand-built container.

- The choice of planting is also completely up to you. You can soften the hard edges of the raised bed with tumbling plants or, if you want a minimalist style, enhance them with a single species to create straight lines formed by vertical plants such as reeds or bamboos. Or go for something modern and not-in-the-least naturalistic with plants such as mosses, balls of Buxus, tufted grasses, or other rounded species, such as thrift. The latter in particular goes very well with a beach theme.

- A very straight and uniform raised bed gives a completely different look. Made out of wood (see page 84), concrete, or metal, it gives a really modern look.

- If you want a more natural but sleek bed, you could try using railway sleepers. Don't buy reclaimed railway sleepers because of the health risks associated with the creosote they are soaked in; instead, get new ones that have been pressure treated (ometimes called tanalized) for an incredibly crisp and fresh look. This kind of timber will turn a pale, washed-out silver after a few years in situ, but you can paint it whatever color you like—perhaps white-washed for a strong minimalist statement—or try growing something tropical in a deep blue or a vibrant red raised bed.

- Raised beds are also excellent for growing your own food and can be filled with herbs and vegetables. Romantics will enjoy growing flowers, and Post-Modernists like foliage and greenery.

DIGGING DOWN

Digging down into the ground to form a pit-like container enables you to create something different again.

The main thing to remember is that by going deeper into the earth, you are more likely to increase the moisture in your container. Water tends to soak downward in our gardens, and the nearer you get to the water table, the more likely you are to find that your beds are saturated a lot of the time. This can be annoying if you're growing Mediterranean herbs, for example, but you can turn this into an asset by growing plants that like to get their feet wet. The technical term for something like this is a *bog garden*. It allows you to grow plants that require permanently damp conditions, such as rushes, sedges, willows, mosses, and reeds. There are some plants, such as *Gunnera macrophylla* (which, in certain countries, such as those of the United Kingdom, cannot be planted near brooks, streams, and the like because it has been deemed invasive, and the flowing water allows the seeds to travel downstream and the plant to colonize natural habitats), that are strikingly architectural but can survive in only the dampest spots. So dig down for a container with a difference.

GOING UP

Wall planters are moving up in the world. Many of us suffer from a chronic lack of growing space, so where can we grow? With ever-increasing residential development in many areas, the first thing to get squeezed is our yards. We want to grow plants and reap the associated benefits, yet we have nowhere to do so.

So what can we do? Well, more and more people are growing upward. "Living" or "green" walls are becoming lifelines for frustrated would-be gardeners the world over, and that means you can get growing even if you have only a wall, a fence, or balcony space. And with the technology in this area getting ever better, there is nothing you can't grow this way, from delicious produce to colorful foliage and flowers.

The main point to keep in mind if you want to embark on vertical planting is that whatever species you choose must not have a vast spread of roots. You want your plants to grow upward but not encroach outward too much; plants have to cram themselves into small spaces, meaning that they cannot produce too big a root system.

There are all kind of ways to create a living wall. The simplest is to use shelving on which you can arrange pots in any way you like. Put the shelves where you want them, plant as many containers as you can with your favorite plants, and arrange them on the shelves (damp and shade-loving plants for a north-facing wall, and drought/sun lovers for a south-facing one). It might be worth considering securing your shelved pots in some way

to stop them from falling off in high winds. You can tie them onto the shelf, run a wire along the front to hold them in place, or hook them onto the shelf itself. Put screws into the shelf, letting them protrude by about 1 inch (2.5 cm), and then hook the containers on top so that the screws go into the drainage holes and hold the pots in place.

If you don't like shelving and want a living wall where you can't see any of the structure that's holding it in place, there are all kinds of systems you can buy. They do vary in price—some are very expensive while others are not. It all depends on what you want to spend and how you want it to look.

You can buy professional pocket systems that hang from the wall with pouches ready to be planted. Simply put in a little soil and then add the desired plants to create an instant green carpet! There are also more inventive, homemade styles that can easily create beautiful green backdrops. You can hang pots on strings, create your own pockets using fabric or wood, or exploit existing cracks in brickwork by using them as planting holes. You can even fashion your own green wall out of wooden pallets (see page 78). If you use one of these

methods, be sure to choose plants that can cope with very dry conditions; for example, you don't want to damage your brickwork by adding too much water to it! If you have a strong, solid wall or fence, you can screw pots to it and plant them.

For the more adventurous, there are countless ways to create a living wall if you are prepared to make something yourself. Hanging pots, making and hanging living frames, and screwing pots to walls are just a few options, and I will go into more detail about these methods in the projects chapter later in the book, but suffice it to say that there are many methods for making your plants go upward and encouraging greenery in places you might not think possible.

HANGING BASKETS

When we think of containers, we often think of hanging baskets. They are wonderful when in their full glory and are favorites among gardeners looking to maximize their planting spaces. The key consideration with a hanging basket is the plants—the wrong plants can ruin the whole effect.

A basket like this is stunning. It takes more than thirty plants and regular feeding, but the results are well worth the effort.

This is not the case with most containers, but the reason you need the right plants for hanging baskets is that usually they have to hide the often not-aesthetically-pleasing containers, so you want plants that hang down to cover the sides and so that the plants can be seen from below. This is why you often find plants like petunias or fuschias in hanging baskets, because they effectively perform both of these tasks, as well as producing pleasing scents, all in one growing season. They are also fairly cheap. But you can be much more adventurous than sticking to petunias; there are other plants, both ornamental and cropping, that will also perform very well in hanging baskets (see page 82).

But don't just focus on the plants if you choose a hanging basket; think about the container, too. You are spoiled for choice in terms of both containers designed for hanging and repurposed or upcycled items. Bird cages are a classic example of an item that can be repurposed into a hanging basket. Any object that can be hung can make an effective feature when enhanced with plants. And there is not even always a need for soil; for the more adventurous gardeners, there are water plants and air plants (see page 106) that get all the nutrients they need from having their roots in water or from gas exchange. Orchids are a prime example; many of these plants naturally grow in trees and get their nutrients from the air around them. Using these types of plants can make a really interesting hanging basket, and excluding soil can be ideal where weight is an issue. If you choose to grow orchids like this, chopped cork makes an excellent growing medium.

WINDOW BOXES

Like hanging baskets, window boxes can have a questionable reputation. Sadly, we have been all-too-frequently exposed to plastic window boxes—cheap plastic at that—possibly in green, imitation terra-cotta, or white. However, there is no reason why this should be the case. If a traditional plastic window box is all you have, and your budget won't allow a terra-cotta or metal trough-type one, you can easily give it a makeover using paint or découpage or by gluing on textured surfaces (see pages 146-151).

Plant your window box with whateverou like—large or small, permanent or seasonal. Whatever it contains, whether bulbs, such as daffodils or tulips; herbs, such as thyme, basil, or parsley; or even a wildflower annual mix that brings the bees buzzing to your window, a container like this will bring beauty and joy every time you look out the window.

MATERIALS

If you grow in containers in a thoughtful way, then you should likewise consider your choice of pot. It is easy to go to a garden center and pick something based on price and convenience, but I urge you to plan and think about which material best lends itself to the kind of feel you want to create in your outdoor space. And don't forget color. White can be modern or traditional, dark colors create a definite look, and bright colors can be exotic or can veer into the childish if not used carefully.

There are ways of changing the look of something or playing with its inherent qualities, either modern or otherwise, by offsetting them with something contrasting (a flowing cottage garden in a steel container, for example), but to guarantee a cohesive look, it is safest to choose a theme and stick to it. This includes the materials of your containers.

PLASTIC

We all know about this material. No matter what it is used for, it cannot really be called "beautiful." Plastic pots have never been the height of horticultural fashion, but nowadays there is a much wider range to choose from, which makes plastic pots more desirable. There are also many ways that you can make them more aesthetically pleasing with just a little effort and imagination, including decorating them with découpage, sand, paint, rope, shells, transfers, or mosaic tiles (see pages 146-151 for ideas).

Rather than thinking of plastic containers as a fashion faux pas, remember the benefits of this material—there are more positive aspects of using plastic pots than you may think.

- The first advantage of classic plastic pots are that they are cheap. You really can't go wrong with them for basic growing, if aesthetics aren't your main objective. You can buy them almost anywhere for next to nothing, and for the thrifty, those in the know, and those into freecycling or recycling, they can often be obtained secondhand or for free. There's a lot to be said for that in a world where everything always costs more than you might think— especially fancy planting containers.

- The second big plus for plastic containers is that they come in a vast range of shapes, sizes, and colors, with drip trays to match. You can also get seed trays, tiny pots, cells (which are also for growing seeds but in their own separate compartments, usually for larger seeds), and plugs. For mass growing and for easy growing, plastic really is the best option.

- The plant lovers out there will appreciate that plastic pots are designed to be very effective at growing plants. That might sound silly, but having worked in nurseries that tried to use alternative materials, I found that there really is no more reliable receptacle for getting plants started. The drainage holes are the right size for holding on to the optimum amount of water while also allowing the pots to release enough liquid to prevent plants from becoming waterlogged. The shiny surface of plastic means that it doesn't crack in cold weather. The pots can be stacked easily and stored en masse without too much hassle, and they are light, making them easy to transport—even with plants growing in them.

As an idealist, if someone were to present me with a pot that was as cheap and effective at producing healthy plants as a plastic one, and that was not detrimental to the environment, I would bite their hand off. But gardeners are also pragmatists; we like to grow plants that will survive and will go on producing for us, without being hampered by bad material. So when needs must, we use products that may not be as carbon neutral and ethically sound as they could be. I personally do not advocate this and so I do try to minimise my use of plastic pots (as well as avoiding spraying chemicals wherever possible and using peat-free compost). For those, like me, who think about these issues, there are now well-supported schemes set up to recycle and reuse plastic pots. I urge you to look these up and to use them wherever possible. That way, the more we grow, the more we reduce our carbon footprint.

The nice thing about wood is that it gives you versatility in terms of design. You can go for a very rustic and earthy look by using materials like driftwood (be aware that different areas have different rules about collecting driftwood) or reclaimed materials such as scaffold planks or similar.

WOOD

When it comes to wood, there is plenty of latitude for creating your own custom containers, and there are also many lovely existing designs.

- The humble wooden container complements more formal garden designs. Traditionally, this style is known as *Italianate*, meaning that it is designed "in the Italian (Renaissance) style," although actually it is now more typified by British and French gardens— so much so that one of the most popular traditional wooden containers has been named the "Versailles planter," which is a square vessel, often decorated with a little ball at the top of each corner post. These are smart-looking and also practical planters, as the traditional designs can slide apart to make repotting, feeding, and renewing soil, as well as tasks like dividing plants, a little easier rather than having to dig or spill out the contents of the container.

- There is also a big "but" with wood, and that is that it rots. You can buy wood that has been pressure treated, which will have a considerably longer life expectancy than untreated, but generally this does not make the most attractive wood. The compromise is that you will have to periodically treat your exterior lumber with preservative or occasionally replace it once it begins to age. However, this deterioration can take many years, so don't write off wood as being too high maintenance. It is a wonderful, versatile, and—if ethically sourced—environmentally sound material.

Alternatively, you can choose a finish that is more refined and genteel. Planed and smoothed hardwoods (any deciduous species like oak or chestnut) make the perfect surface for your plants to dangle against in raised beds. You can also buy a prefabricated container made of this type of wood, or, for a very sleek finish, you could build the planters into the rest of your hard landscaping, incorporating them into raised decking, for example, or to act as dividing walls.

There is a vast range of choice when it comes to clay. The colors, shapes, sizes, and styles vary, and, unlike most other kinds of pots, there are some more functional options available. Sadly, for those of us who try to be a little thrifty, clay pots have become artisan items and often come with high price tags. However, there are still bargains out there. I recently picked up a bunch of clay containers from a friend who'd closed her nursery business. She had hundreds of small terra-cotta pots that she wanted to get rid of, so I gave them a happy home.

STONEWARE & EARTHENWARE

Clay containers are extremely popular choices. The word "pot" itself, which is so frequently used to describe containers, comes from the word "pottery," and there are many good reasons for this material being a longtime favorite.

- The first is that it is so durable; it can cope with heat, cold, wet, dry, wind, rain, and basically any condition you choose to throw at it. There are some clays that might crack in very cold and wet weather because water that has soaked into the pores expands as it freezes, but generally a clay pot will be able to withstand most, if not all, weather conditions.

- A great way to get inspiration is to look at your neighbors' houses and gardens to see what they have, and then ask them where they got their pots. It's also a nice way to get to know your neighbors—though don't blame me if you regret this later!

- You may remember the blue pots that dominated TV screens and garden centers for many years, and I still have a soft spot for them. I love the rich color of lapis lazuli, but glazes come in such a variety of shades that there is plenty of choice. Take a look at your local garden center—this range will be just the tip of the iceberg. There are stores that specialize in pots of all kinds, and there are also independent pottery artists that produce containers, sometimes to order, and often for surprisingly little money. So shop around in your local area and see what you can find.

Even just a small selection of the types of clay pots available shows the variety of choice for all colors, shapes, sizes, and positions in the garden.

I would not normally recommend a plantless container but will happily make an exception for fire! If a fire pit is something you want in your yard—and, after all, a fire pit is essentially a container for fire—then stone is the ideal material. Metal is really the only other option.

STONE

Unlike terra-cotta, stone pots tend to put greater weight on aesthetics than practicality; in other words, don't look for little versions to grow your seedlings in. But stone pots are usually very beautiful.

- Stone pots come in both rustic and extremely modern forms, and there is a movement toward marble-like but matte-finished carved pots—the likes of which would have graced the Parthenon, but without the fussy decoration. Stone containers tend to be on the large side, too, and this craftsmanship and scale often come with hefty price tags.

- However, there is no denying that the beauty of a carved piece of stone is captivating and gives importance and weight to a garden's design. Because of its potential size and grandeur, a stone container can feel like part of the furniture—part of the very make-up of the space—and can help bring together a design. For example, it can blend in with or complement hard landscaping, such as a patio or walls, so the containers feel like part of the design rather than an afterthought.

- Stone containers are not limited to the large and grandiose. The rustic look never goes out of fashion if it looks intentionally rustic, and there is always a huge range of such containers to choose from. They are often smaller than their elegant, smooth equivalents, which makes them ideal for more modest-sized gardens.

- If the price of real stone makes this option unfeasible, there are more modestly priced concrete alternatives. Many of them are made from the same or similar molds as their stone counterparts, so, for all intents and purposes, they have the same look.

If you want to really integrate stone containers into your garden, why not build them yourself? You can make containers in walls by leaving gaps for planting on the top surface. If you are building the walls yourself, or having them built by a builder or landscaper, you can design them however you like, in any color, texture, shape, width, and height. You can make them smooth and modern, or rustic, or even use a dry stone wall to both contain your plants and to grow other small plants in the little crevices between the stones.

However you plant them, containers made from brick or stone provide a fantastic opportunity to seamlessly incorporate plants into design and also to use them for what designers and gardeners have been using them for for centuries—to soften the hard lines of landscaping materials.

METAL

Metal is an increasingly popular choice for containers. It can come in a range of shapes, sizes, and colors and gives an industrial feel and a modernist look. But metal can also be a beautiful and unpredictable material as it ages, reacting with the elements to form bubbles, imperfections, and bold colors.

If you like a metal container because of the way it looks at that time and want it to stay that way, there are many metals that will remain crisp and fresh in appearance. And (let's get down to the dull stuff) they are really easy to clean. So if that's appealing to you, look for galvanized steel, which will not weather at all. There are some inexpensive bucket-style containers and other pots made of metal that are quite utilitarian, and they are a good alternative to plastic without being overpriced. They also give an upcycled look without you actually having to do any work at all.

- The brilliant thing about many metals is that they age so attractively; as the seasons pass and the weather has its effects, they change color and patina and, unlike many other materials, often improve with age. The obvious example is iron, which turns a vivid burnt orange, but think also of copper steeples on old churches and their gorgeous, aged-green color or the russet hues of oxidized brass.

- If you are a fan of the aged-metal look but not its capricious nature, look into containers made from corten steel, which has a uniform rusting effect that looks both modern and aged. It's increasingly popular and well worth investigating.

- Another advantage of metal is its magnetic quality, and you can buy magnetic pots. They aren't cheap, but they are pretty amazing. This material is great when used as mini herb-growing containers that you can stick on the fridge or metal walls or other surfaces in the garden (see page 96). This allows you to make a really simple living wall without having to mount brackets and frames, so the pots can be easily replaced or revitalized throughout the year when they grow too leggy or when you just feel like a change. It also gives your living wall the flexibility for pots to be moved according to how well the plants are doing; if one plant is being hammered by the wind, you can move it to a lower position. Or if a plant is being affected by the shade, you can move it up so it gets more sun.

If you're using a metal container that will age, always remember to treat the inside so that rust does not turn the soil too acidic. And drill some holes in the bottom!

GLASS

You might not immediately think about putting glass containers in your garden (we naturally think of glass as being delicate and brittle), but its merits are becoming increasingly appreciated and, when you think about it, it makes perfect sense. We've used glass in the garden for centuries—as cloches, greenhouses, cold frames, and many more features.

- These practical uses have become quite outdated, but I believe that we should use glass as a staple material for outdoor growing. Glass is strong, and, with reinforced or tempered glass, it is becoming even more versatile. If you have small children, though, think carefully about using a lot of glass containers, particularly if they are not made from shatterproof glass; otherwise, there should be nothing stopping you from using it.

- Glass is not as strong as stone or as flexible as metal, but it is not much different to clay in its make-up, and it has one very interesting quality that clay does not: it is clear. This opens new doors for growers in terms of the species they can grow and the looks they can achieve.

- We tend to use containers in a fairly single-minded way: we fill them with soil and grow plants at the surface. This is because if we put the plants too deep in the pot, they miss out on a key requirement: light. So materials like clay limit your growing capabilities, unless you're using it for a very specific purpose, such as excluding light to force rhubarb in the spring. With glass containers, this problem is eliminated; your containers can become miniature glasshouses. This creates a mini microclimate; the light lets in heat in the form of reacting photons (particles of light), which increases humidity and allows you to grow plants outside that you could never have grown before, including tropical and subtropical species.

- With modern-day sustainability in mind, this leads us to another reason for using glass containers, and that is as a means of recycling. We go through so much glass in our homes: as bottles and jars for beer, wine, jelly, honey, water and other drinks, and spices and herbs. You can recycle these items at recycling centers or in the correct recycling bins, but you can also reuse them in slightly more creative ways by upcycling them. Used in this way, old glass can make beautiful and very simple containers, either traditionally as pots or as terrariums, and make great gifts.

- If the clarity of the material is a good reason for using glass, then I'd like to advocate clarity of the substrate, too—the soil substitute. Many plants grow simply in water, from which they can get all of their nutrients. If these plants are also grown in glass containers, it creates a really interesting opportunity to see the workings of the plants and the ecosystem that surrounds them— you can appreciate the roots in a way you've never seen before. It's a great educational tool for children as well as being visually interesting, especially if combined with some sort of lighting positioned behind it.

- And for those practical growers out there, don't think that growing in water and glass is reserved for weird and wonderful water-loving species; many edible crops like lettuce, leeks, and onions can be grown in just water. Simply leave the roots intact— or the base of the plants if there are no roots left—and stick them in old jelly jars on the windowsill.

POND POTS

Container ponds can be any shape, size, or style that you want them to be. They can be made from pots or tanks; in plastic, glass, metal, brick, or stone; and be square, round, hexagonal, sunken, or raised. They can be all of these things and still be great for wildlife, for an informal theme, or if you want more modern-looking features. Having a pond pot also provides the opportunity to grow a whole range of water-loving plants that you couldn't ordinarily grow in a run-of-the-mill container.

GROUPS OF POTS

Using many containers together is a very traditional yet incredibly effective way of displaying plants. This type of container gardening has had somewhat of a renaissance, but with a slightly different spin. The group does not have to be two-dimensional; by using containers of different sizes and shapes, and platforms to elevate some, you can add height and multiple layers to your display, which is a great design tool, especially in a small space.

- One simple way to create temporary impact in a garden that can be repeated in your next garden (if you move) is to group together a tasteful display of three or maybe five pots (always work in groups of odd numbers). The pots could be the same color (or shades of the same color; see left) or a variety, depending on the look you want to create, and usually look best in a variety of sizes.

- Plant them with minimal, usually monochromatic (green and one other color), plants for a tasteful display. Red and green create a bold statement, whereas green and pastels like pale blues, pinks, lilacs, or soft yellows, or even white, create something more subtle. You could even choose green and a paler green for something ultramodern, or green and black (or as black as can be in the plant world—usually a very dark purple) for a striking look. Herbs such as thyme and rosemary look particularly lovely, as well as being tasty and evergreen to boot!

Here, retro '90s blue-glazed pots en masse have been given a new lease on life with some bold, bright flowers.

For more confident and adventurous plants, move away from monochrome and into multicolor. Here, a tropical feel is created with canna lilies, dahlias, katsura, fuchsias, salvia, and hostas, using complementary foliage and flower color.

THE POTS

43

With patience, you can create a truly breathtaking display of pots using a huge range of species. It's great for plant collectors, making it easy to replace plants as needed or as desired.

HOW TO...

Get the groundwork right, and growing in a container is easy. Planting in a pot is mostly common sense, but there are a few tricks of the trade that will make your plants infinitely happier in their little homes. This, in turn, will make caring for your plants much easier.

In this chapter, I will take you through the different stages of creating your containers and the different options to consider at each stage to make your pots both functional and stunning.

FIRST THINGS FIRST: THE POT ITSELF

Think of a container as its own little ecosystem. You have the ground (that's the soil), the animals (the microbes, worms, and bugs that live in the soil), and the plant life (whatever you choose to grow in your pot). In a normal ecosystem, these components are infinitely complex, ever-changing, and bigger than you will find in your miniature, container-sized ecosystem. In a garden, you get an idea of what it is to create a real habitat with numerous complex layers of organisms acting with and upon each other, creating a fluctuating world that more or less takes care of itself. This is not so in a container, and that is the main thing you need to understand if you want to be a successful container gardener, particularly when it comes to nurturing your plants.

The basic principle of container gardening is that you are taking a small part of an ecosystem and isolating it. You might have patches in your garden that are shady, sunny, dry, damp, windy, sheltered, frosty or protected in winter and every variation in between—all in the one space. In a container, this is not the case; you have little to no diversity. If you have a container that suits a drought-tolerant plant, then every plant in that pot must be drought tolerant. In this sense, particularly for beginners or those who like to keep things simple, this makes your job easy. On the other hand, the lack of natural fluctuation removes a certain degree of the force of nature. In a monoculture or very simplified mini-ecosystem, you lack the natural buildup of nutrients that you would find in a wild ecosystem. Similarly, there will not be as many worms and microbes to enrich the soil. Remember the second reason in chapter 1: you can always move a container if it's not doing well!

The big positive is that in a container you have ultimate control over what you grow and where. However, you also have a big responsibility because the survival of that plant in that pot depends almost solely on you. So how do you get this unique relationship between pot, plant, and person to thrive? Well, there isn't one easy formula; essentially, it is up to you to provide the optimal conditions.

There are five key things that every plant needs to survive:

- Water (in varying amounts).
- Air (both above and below the ground).
- Nutrients (different requirements for different plants, but essentially the same twelve nutrients in different measures [see page 56]).
- Temperature (different temperatures for different species).
- Light (again in varying amounts).

The first thing to consider when choosing or making a pot is its size. This is key for whatever plant you want to grow. Certain plants, like *Agapanthus* and strawberries, need very little root space and can cope well with their roots being restricted, while others, like figs and hops, will accept being in a pot but would really do better in the ground. In such cases, the bigger the container, the better. But remember, the pot must also fit in the space you have.

Once you've considered these things, you should have a rough idea of the size of pot you need. If you have the container already and have assessed its size, you need to decide what kinds of plants you can put in it. For instance, if you discover a tea tin for less than the price of a cup of tea in a thrift shop, you're not going to try to wedge an apple tree into it—that's just common sense. Instead, you might think about going smaller and more compact, perhaps along the lines of some pea shoots, watercress, herbs, or a strawberry plant. If you're more into flowers, an alpine, like saxifrage or *Raoulia,* would do very well.

If you have a huge urn or a trough, you can use it for a much larger plant— perhaps even a tree. A Japanese maple makes a nice feature for a container, or try growing a cherry, plum, or pear tree if you want to grow your own fruit. Or— and this is where there is almost endless opportunity for flair and creativity—you could fill the pot with a whole host of different species to make a beautiful display. Flowers of complementary colors and similar requirements live in harmony in one container, or, if you're partial to a more restrained palette, you could have different species in just a single color. If you're a minimalist, you could even fill a large container with one species for a simple, clean, and muted look.

MATERIAL

The second consideration is the material that your container is made of. There is a slight difference in which plants suit which materials.

PLASTIC, with its shiny surface, is really good for plants that like high levels of moisture because it holds in water, not allowing it to seep through the sides.

TERRA-COTTA (unglazed) works well with species that like free-draining soil and cope well with hot roots because the pores in the material allow water to be released and keep the soil cooler. If the terra-cotta is glazed, especially on the inside, it doesn't allow for seepage and will be much better for water lovers.

METAL is a tricky material for a container, even though it may look great, because of its tendency to get extremely hot in the sun. There are few, if any, plants that really enjoy having their roots get very hot. For example, a clematis will simply turn up its toes and refuse to flower if its roots begin to bake. However, there are some plants, often corms (specialized storage roots similar to bulbs), that need "baking" in order to flower, and they are usually planted with their roots exposed to the sunlight. Flag irises are a classic example of this. These types of flowers can cope in metal containers as long as there is enough soil between the metal edges and the roots themselves. But, generally, if you really want to use metal containers, it is wisest to put another (preferably plastic) container inside the metal one to reduce the amount of heat conducted through the soil, thus protecting the plant inside.

WOODEN containers are fairly versatile, but because they are usually lined with a plastic or butyl liner to prevent the wood from rotting, they do lend themselves to plants that like to get their feet wet. However, armed with a drill, you can pierce several drainage holes into the base of the liner to make a good receptacle for plants that prefer drier conditions.

There are, of course, containers available that are made from many other materials that are too numerous to list here, but I've tried to cover the most common types. Whichever material you use, be are aware of one key requirement: drainage holes.

DRAINAGE

Drainage is a very important part of container gardening. More plants are killed through overwatering than underwatering, especially in today's unpredictable climate. So it is crucial that your containers get the right amount of water.

Generally, with most plants, you need to include at least one large, or several small, drainage holes in the base of your container. Think of the standard black plastic pot that your plants come in from the garden center, which have several holes in the bottom—that gives you an indication of how well drained most plants need to be. As ugly and environmentally unfriendly as those pots may be, they are arguably the most effective receptacles for growing plants.

It is important to get the right amount of drainage for specific plants, so be aware of the needs of the plants you are using. There are many plant species that need a lot of water; for example, bog gardens have become more popular, encouraging people to grow plants that thrive in a waterlogged or permanently moist environment. If you decide to make a bog-garden container, put one small drainage hole in the bottom, just to make sure the soil doesn't get completely waterlogged and toxic—but only one; otherwise, the drainage will be too effective and therefore unsuitable for the species you want to grow. If you

are making a pond in a pot, there is no need for any drainage holes at all. In fact, if you do put them in, rather than a glorious haven for aquatic plants, you are more likely to have to file a claim on your homeowners' insurance, or at least get complaints from the downstairs neighbors, when the contents flood out!

Another good way to improve drainage is by using pieces of stone or, more commonly, broken-up pieces of hard clay or pottery that go in the bottom of your container before you add the growing medium.

How much of this material you need depends on the conditions that your plant prefers. Obviously, the more drought tolerant your plant is, the more stones or pieces of pottery it will need in the container, but even moisture-loving plants should have a few pieces in the base of the pot because they serve to stop the buildup of wet, sloppy soil that becomes full of pathogens and toxicity due to waterlogging. No plant likes that kind of moisture; even in a pond pot, you will need to include oxygenating plants to get air to the roots of the aquatic plants. A sloppy base of soil will do nothing but harm. So sticking a few stones or pieces of broken pottery in the base of the pot gets the water moving through the soil quickly once it gets down to a deeper level in the container. They can also cover the holes in the pot to make the soil inside less likely to fall through the drainage holes when you water. So it's win-win.

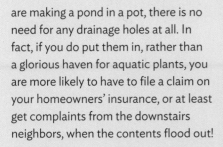

SOIL

The next consideration (and now we are really into the nitty-gritty) is the soil that you use. This is where things start to get a little more complex. Unlike all the other steps, it is not just a case of choosing your soil and letting the plants do their thing. Whatever growing medium you choose will need to be replenished on an annual or biennial basis to keep plants thriving (see page 152).

In technical circles, we use the term "growing medium" or "substrate" rather than "soil," simply because a lot of plants don't necessarily like a soil-based medium. The pond in a trough (page 106), for example, uses water as its substrate, whereas something like an orchid grows best in chopped-up cork. Get the substrate right, and you are more than halfway to success. If in doubt, consider it a general rule that most plants like a neutral to slightly acidic soil.

SOIL TYPES SIMPLIFIED

Acid lovers	Ericaceous soil
Edibles (fruit and vegetables)	Nutrient-rich soil (with manure)
Edibles (herbs)	Free-draining soil with sand or gravel added
Seeds and cuttings	Low-nutrient soil
Conifers	Slightly acidic soil
Water lovers	Humus-rich soil
Aquatics	Water
Orchids	Cork or bark
Cacti, succulents and drought lovers	Free-draining soil with a lot of sand or gravel

Soil mixes can create some differing opinions. For many generations, we have used peat as our principal growing medium for a number of reasons. First, it is very good at retaining moisture without getting waterlogged. Second, it is low in nutrients, which means that you can add whichever nutrients the particular plants you are growing will need, tailoring it to their exact requirements. There are, however, some rather dramatic drawbacks to some soil blends. Peat is an endangered and ever-decreasing material; peat bogs take thousands of years to form and are unique environments. Despite much research, scientists have found it impossible to recreate the conditions in which peat develops. The bottom line is that we are eating into a finite resource when we add peat to soil, so it is worth investigating the available peat-free alternatives, which I always try to use wherever possible.

However, there are also objections to some of the alternatives. Coir, for example, is a great peat-free growing medium that is a waste product from the coconut industry, but it is often associated with less-than-fair-trade working conditions and, of course, high air miles.

Another, fairly obvious, alternative to peat is a soil-based compost. This is a great option because you can produce it yourself by mixing your own garden soil or bought topsoil with compost and composted leaves, which makes it a cheap option. The only drawback is that its drainage levels vary, depending on what type of soil you have or the kind of soil-based compost you buy. You may have to improve the drainage by adding something from the "soil additives'" section (see page 54).

Something that I use often and really like as a basic container growing medium, is a compost made from cattail (bulrush). It's light and free draining, and it grows healthy specimens. It is a very sutiable alternative to peat because it is a completely renewable resource.

So there you have the minefield that is choosing your growing medium. Now what do you do with it?

ADDITIVES

There are many substances you can add to your soil at this stage of planting your container that will make your plants healthier and, crucially, make your life easier in the long term. So what are these additives and what do they do?

GRAVEL OR SAND

As someone who has had to empty many a waterlogged pot that sat in its own juices for months on end, I can tell you that it is not a fun job! This issue can be easily avoided by adding a little bit of sand or a few scoops of gravel. Neither material will harm your plants, and adding it could pay dividends in the future. For plants that need a lot of drainage, such as bulbs—lilies, in particular—and Mediterranean plants, such as *geraniums*, thyme, and lavender, make the soil and gravel/sand mix a 50:50 split. The compost retains moisture and nutrients and gives the plant's roots a good structure to hold on to, while the sand or gravel allows the free movement of water around the roots and stops waterlogging. For less drought-tolerant species, add a few scoopfuls of gravel or sand just to help your plants out. If you have a bog pot or pond pot, then keep the gravel to a minimum. Succulents and cacti can be grown in gravel with just a little soil added.

WATER RETAINERS

The next additive that you can use is something that helps containers hold on to their moisture. Water-retaining additives come in all shapes and sizes. For example, some are like clear glass marbles made out of gel that slowly release their moisture and then shrink, and there are water-retaining crystals that look like crystalline salts and swell when you water your containers, slowly releasing their liquid over a period of time, meaning that you need to water less frequently. They work very well for hanging baskets or pots that are hard to get to, or you can add them to your pots if you are going away on a short trip. The easiest way to use these little beads of moisture is to add them to the soil as you are making up your containers. That way, you won't cause any root damage by digging into the pot later, when the plants have established themselves.

PERLITE & VERMICULITE

They may sound more like ways to kill Superman than items to use in your garden, but, trust me, perlite and vermiculite are wonderful. Perlite is exploded volcanic glass—a bit like pumice, but heated to incredibly high temperatures. These little bits of rock are totally inert, meaning they contain neither nutrients nor anything harmful. They hold moisture because of all of the air that's been introduced to the rock in the heating process, but they do little else. That is why perlite is so good for growing cuttings: it allows the stems to root without overfeeding, which can lead to weak growth. It is also a good soil amendment because it increases drainage and adds moisture retention.

Perlite is also astoundingly light, making it a great addition or alternative to gravel or sand in a hanging basket or window box that you do not want to be too heavy for structural reasons. It is completely natural, so it does not compromise any organic principles you might have, although there is a little energy required to heat the rock in the first place as well as some air miles associated with its import. Overall, it is a relatively cheap, easy, and effective way of improving your compost. Try a 50:50 mix with a multipurpose soil for general use in a container and with soil for seeds and cuttings. Otherwise, try a 50:25:25 mix with half soil, a quarter gravel or sand, and a quarter perlite. If the plants that you are growing are particularly moisture loving, don't overdo the perlite.

Vermiculite is a similar product to perlite and is used in a similar way. It is incredibly light and holds on to moisture, but it also contains air, so it allows some gas exchange in the soil. It is made from hydrated minerals and, because it is so light, it is often used to top-dress the soil, particularly in seed containers, covering the seed with a light layer of moisture-retentive particles. It doesn't have the same structural integrity as perlite, so it gets squashed down into much smaller particles and breaks down quite quickly in the soil. That is not a bad thing— it's just different from the tenacious perlite. Essentially, both perlite and vermiculite will do the same job, but one will do it for longer than the other.

FERTILIZERS

You will need to add fertilizer to your containers throughout their lifetime. The easiest time to add fertilizer is when you first plant your pots, because that is the most effective way of dispersing it evenly throughout the soil. This way, the roots—both existing ones and potential new ones—will be fertilized equally. So mix the fertilizer with your soil or compost, along with your gravel or perlite or sand (or all three) and and any other additives, and then put it in your container along with your plant or plants. Simple(ish)!

NUTRIENTS

But what fertilizer do you use? There are twelve essential plant nutrients that will almost always be present in whatever fertilizer you add to the soil, as well as in smaller quantities in the soil itself and in compost. These nutrients are:

Nitrogen
Phosphorus
Potassium
Sulphur
Magnesium
Calcium
Iron
Boron
Manganese
Zinc
Molybdenum
Copper

Of these twelve nutrients, there are three that plants need in considerably higher quantities than the rest, and they will be represented on the fertilizer's packaging in the form of a ratio. The nutrients are usually listed in the following order: N (nitrogen): P (phosphorus): K (potassium). These are known as primary nutrients. The rest of the nutrients will not be shown on the packaging because plants need them in such miniscule quantities.

So what do those three major nutrients do? Well, **nitrogen** is needed by the leaves of the plant. If you are growing a shrub or a herbaceous plant that is grown more for its leaves than for its flowers, or a leafy vegetable, choose a fertilizer with a higher level of N. If you are using natural fertilizers this will be a substance like manure; chicken manure in particular is noted for its high nitrogen levels.

Phosphorus is needed by roots, so any plant with a weak root system that must be built up, or one that has tubers, rhizomes, or any kind of storage root, such as dahlias or root vegetables, will need higher levels of phosphorus.

Potassium is required by the reproductive parts of a plant: the flowers and the fruits. For any plant that's grown solely for its fruits or for its flowers, use a fertilizer with a high level of potassium. For a natural version, seaweed, wood fire ash, and bat manure are particularly good.

It's important to note that all plants need all three of these nutrients, plus many more, and nearly all fertilizers are higher in nitrogen than any other element. That is OK; don't be put off by a certain fertilizer because it is high in nitrogen when you need something with high potassium, for example. Just look for the product that has the highest potassium level while keeping in mind it will still have more nitrogen than anything else.

TYPES OF FERTILIZER

There are all kinds of fertilizers on the market, but they are all divided into two distinct groups: slow release and quick release. A slow-release fertilizer stays in the container for a number of weeks or months and seeps its nutrients slowly into the growing medium, providing a sustained feeding system. A quick-release fertilizer provides, as the name suggests, an immediate rush of nutrients. It gives a boost when it's needed and then is gone just days later. Both types can be natural or synthetic, and organic or inorganic. I tend to stick to the organic kinds whenever possible. These usually take the form of manure (either horse—which is easiest to come by—cow or chicken), which needs to age for six months to a year before it can be mixed into your compost. Essentially, this just means that you leave the manure outside, usually (but not always) covered, until the toxic compounds, such as ammonia, have broken down to be replaced with usable compounds, like nitrates.

Another organic fertilizer is bonemeal: dried fish, blood, and bone. This is a granular fertilizer that you can mix with the soil or scatter immediately around the roots of plants. It is technically a quick-release fertilizer, rapidly dissolved and absorbed, but it hangs around in the soil for a few weeks, if not months.

It is worth noting at this point that the more free draining your soil, the quicker the fertilizer you add to it will be washed away. So you must strike a balance. For the perfect combination, aim for a soil that is free draining but (and this is the crucial part) moisture retentive, unless your plant has special requirements.

Finally, a super quick-release fertilizer, and one that I use a lot, is comfrey tea. It is free to make if you have comfrey growing in your garden, or it can be foraged with the landowner's permission. It is worth growing a pot of comfrey just to guarantee a constant supply of this precious liquid (see right)! It works like tomato feed or liquid seaweed, and you add it to your watering can.

For comfrey growers who want longer-lasting results, cut the leaves and dig them into or lay them on top of the soil. This makes a slow-release version of comfrey-tea fertilizer.

The aforementioned are all organic options, but if you go to a garden center, you will also be able to find inorganic versions. Slow-release fertilizers usually come in pellet form and release their goodness into the soil over two to three months.

Although it can be tempting to pile it on when applying fertilizer, always read the instructions on the package and err on the side of caution. Overfeeding plants, far from saving you time, can actually cause damage by either stunting them badly or, in the worst case, killing them altogether. More is not always better when it comes to fertilizer; a healthy balance is best.

COMFREY TEA RECIPE

To make comfrey tea, remove the leaves from the comfrey plant and immerse them in a bucket of water, stirring the concoction every few days for two months. You might want to place a large stone on top to keep the leaves submerged. Do beware of the smell—it is potent. It's a good idea to cover the bucket with a lid and perhaps place it in a less-used part of your yard. After two months, dilute the comfrey tea into your watering can at a ratio of one part comfrey tea to ten parts water and then use it to spot-feed plants.

ALTERNATIVE MANURES

There are many other manures available, but they can be more difficult to get your hands on. Bat manure is incredibly high in potassium, so if you know a bat conservation society or anyone who has bat boxes, it may  be worth befriending them. Alpaca manure is also highly sought after. There are alpaca farms springing up all over the place, and the manure is ripe for the picking. The great thing about alpaca manure is that you don't need to age it at all—it can go straight from posterior to pot, so to speak. Just make sure that you wear gloves when you handle it.

MULCH

Mulching is one of the last jobs you need to do when planting containers. It is optional but worth doing. Mulch can be a strange concept for nongardeners; it is basically a layer of material that lies on the top of the soil, but it serves a good purpose.

Mulch is designed to make your life easier and is surprisingly effective. It keeps weeds at bay by preventing light from getting to the soil, which stops weeds from gaining strength. It also stops your containers from losing too much water, which means you can water less often. Plus, it looks much more attractive than bare soil.

You don't *need* to add mulch—the plants will not die without it—but when growing in containers that you want to be aesthetically pleasing, it really does help finish them off.

Gravel usually provides the nicest look, but you can also use bark, matting, or even soil, which will feed the plants over time, too.

DRIP TRAY

Once your container is finished, with all the features such as drainage, fertilizer, mulch, and the plant itself in place, all that's left to do is water it. And here's where a drip tray comes in handy.

A drip tray is a container that catches any excess water that runs through the soil and out of the pot's drainage holes, and there are a few good reasons for using one. One reason is to protect any surfaces your container is perched on—such as decking, a balcony, a windowsill, or concrete—by preventing water from sitting around the base of your container for long periods. Having a drip tray also allows you to water less frequently, because any water that flows through the soil in the container will sit in the drip tray and get slowly pulled back up by the plant's roots through capillary action—the roots suck up the water like a straw. This has obvious benefits for the environment, too, because it means lthat ess water is wasted. However, be careful not to overwater your plants; in general, plants do not like to sit in moisture all the time, so make sure your drip trays aren't always full of water.

As well as being really practical, drip trays can also be attractive. Often they may sit at the bases of pots and are pretty innocuous, but there are trays that completely cover your pots, meaning that you can pot plants in any old container and then hide them entirely with a lovely, ornate drip tray.

Handy and practical—that's a combination that you should never underestimate!

If your pot is very big, and you don't want to ruin the floor, or if you have a very ornate floor and are worried that the pot itself will cause damage, then placing your pot on a structure that lifts it off the ground can be a good idea.

PROJECTS

Whether you go to your local garden center or home-improvement store, you will find that although there is a wide range of containers ready to buy, the truly inspiring ideas often come with hefty price tags. However, there is no reason why you cannot create your own personalized containers or use available containers in clever ways to fit into your garden design. From pottery to pallets, there are cheap and easy ways of making any size or shape of container as well as innovative, decorative ways to display pots.

Remember that in one container, all of the plants will be subject to the same conditions. I have created projects that will grow well together and can be adapted. Just make sure that if you plant more than one species together, they all require the same growing conditions.

1

BRIGHT DISPLAYS ON A LADDER

🕐 **AN AFTERNOON**

An old wooden stepladder makes a great prop and a clever space-saving device to show off your most prized potted plants. A rustic old set of steps becomes exciting when offset by the striking use of a modern color palette of plants. I have used bright colors to make this feel a little more tropical and edgy, but it would work equally well with a cottage-garden theme in pastel colors. You could paint the ladder a neutral or dark color, like navy blue, to offset the bright plants, but for added heat, try a splash of bold paint—royal blue, bright red, or orange. Or, if you have the space (and the ladders), all three together could look fantastic when crammed with plants! Or just paint the pots!

YOU WILL NEED

An old wooden stepladder
Exterior multisurface paint in
    your favorite color (optional)
Brackets and bolts for securing
    the ladder to the wall or floor
A lot of terra-cotta pots (various
    sizes are fine)
Soil
An exciting mix of bright-colored
    plants and contrasting plants
Try a second set of display pots
    for the winter months,
    focusing more on foliage
    and evergreen species such as
    evergreen ferns, *Ruscus,
    Skimmia, Vinca, Phormium,*
    conifer species, or evergreen
    grasses

METHOD

1. If painting the ladder, do so first.
2. Place the ladder where you intend to display it. The plants should be the main focus, so think about the backdrop carefully. A neutral wall will enhance the floral display. Also think about the ladder's placement in practical terms; you don't want to be tripping over it and creating a terra-cotta mess, so put it where it can be easily seen but doesn't interfere with any activities.
3. Attach it to either the wall or the floor in order to ensure it stays securely in place. Use brackets that attach to the ladder and the wall or floor and bolt into place securely.
4. Half-fill the pots with compost and then add the bright-colored plants and contrasting plants of purple or silver—the more pots, the more impact your display will have. For a modern feel, keep pots to a neat minimum; choose a certain number per shelf and stick to it. For example, three works well because odd numbers always look more pleasing.
5. Arrange the pots so that the tallest plants are not impinging too much on the plants above. Make sure the color arrangement is balanced, with bright colors evenly spread out. The plants on the top rungs will probably get more intense sunlight than the those on the lower rungs.
6. Water regularly. Feed flowering or even fruiting plants such as geraniums, tomatoes, peppers, marigolds, black-eyed Susans, and dahlias throughout the season with a high-potassium liquid feed.

**A gorgeous mix of
bright-colored plants**
Red hot pokers
Verbena
Geraniums
Begonia
Black-eyed Susans
Zinnia
Gazania
Crocosmia
Dahlias
Helenium
Elymus
Salvia
Lobelia cardinalis
Papaver
Hedera helix 'Goldheart'
Thunbergia alata
   (these last two are
   great for cascades)
Echinacea

Contrasting plants
Bright colors can be
a bit much unless
tempered with
something that offers
a relief for the
eye. Try:
Purple sage
Allium
Senecio cineraria
Melianthus major
Purple cabbage
Lavender
Salvia nemorosa
Perovskia
Eryngium
Artemisia

2

OLD PALLET WITH OLIVE TREES

🕐 **AN AFTERNOON**

Be careful when selecting your pallets because the blocks that separate the two frames are sometimes made of solid wood and other times of reconstituted wood pulp. Some are already broken, others not, and some have tops with no gaps, which means there's more good wood to be used.

Also remember that pallet wood is never pressure treated, so you will need to either treat it yourself or think carefully about what you plant in it—never plant anything that requires a lot of water, and place the container somewhere that avoids a lot of rainfall. This is why I have chosen an olive tree to plant in this container; it can cope with full sun and some wind, and it needs very little water—perfect for a pallet.

YOU WILL NEED

Protective clothing, including
    gloves and goggles
Shovel/crowbar
A pallet or two (You will need
    to cover the sides of a box at least
    12 inches [about 30 cm] cubed.
    You can cut the wood off the
    framework of your pallets or you
    can pry them off and cut them to
    size, in which case you will need
    fewer pallets.)
Saw
Hammer
Screws and screwdriver
Staple gun
Permeable membrane or liner
Washed horticultural sand
Multipurpose soil
Olive tree
Landscape rock
Gravel mulch (optional)

METHOD

1. Using your shovel, pry the pallet wood apart until you have separated the planks from the supporting framework. This can be a tricky process; for best results, put your pallet on a stable surface. If this is too difficult, and the wood splits before it comes off the pallet, cut the wood off its framework, but be aware that this will give you much shorter planks.

2. Hammer any nails out of the wood so that it is safe to handle.

3. Construct a cube from the thicker supporting lumber originally used for the frame of the pallet. The cube must be big enough to hold the root ball of your tree and preferably at least a third bigger to give the roots room to grow (usually at least 12 inches [30 cm] cubed).

4. Cut the pallet planks to a length that's just above the height of your cube and then screw them to the cube you've made—they can be horizontal or vertical, depending on your personal preference.

5. Screw the pallet planks to the underside of your cube, making sure that you leave gaps between them for any water to escape through.

6. Turn the cube the right way up and then, using a staple gun, attach the liner to the inside of the container.

7. Mix the gravel with the soil in either a 50:50 mix or with slightly more gravel than soil.

8. Put a few inches of gritty soil in the bottom of the container. Place your olive tree in the container and fill all the gaps around it with the remaining soil. Water well and then top off with landscape rock.

13 GREAT ALTERNATIVES TO AN OLIVE

Rock rose
Chaenomeles speciosa
Nandina domestica
Abelia x grandiflora
Olearia macrodonta
Elaeagnus ebbingei
Eucalyptus gunnii
Koelreuteria paniculata
Cercis siliquastrum
Callistemon citrinus
Acacia dealbata
Melianthus major
Sorbus aria

3

PRAIRIE-INSPIRED UPCYCLED METAL BIN

For an alternative, use *Eupatorium rugosum* 'Chocolate' and *Panicum virgatum* 'Heavy Metal.'

AN HOUR

The prairie style is a contemporary planting theme that has become popular in the last few decades. It uses a lot of greens, particularly grasses, but offsets them with flowers that are naturally found in prairies and savannahs. As well as being stylish, it is also a very low-maintenance design that will cope with most conditions, so it really is a win-win, especially when combined with a tasteful container. Some grasses are also evergreen, providing year-round interest, which is always a bonus.

For this project, I am using metal as a contemporary material to pair with the planting, though you could use any type of container. When using metal it is important to put a membrane between the container and the soil to prevent the plants' roots overheating and scorching, as metal gets very hot.

TIP: Add bulbs for year-round interest.

I've used:
Grasses *Carex morrowii* (variegated) and *Miscanthus sinensis*
Flowers Chocolate cosmos (*Cosmos atrosanguineus*), but any plant with a traditional daisy-like flower will give a prairie feel.

PRAIRIE PLANTER IDEAS

Annual prairie—Annual poppy with *Panicum elegans* and *Cosmos*.

Purple and yellow prairie—*Stipa gigantea, Echinacea, Verbena bonariensis* and *Stipa tenuissima*.

Daisy flower prairie—*Echinacea purpurea, Rudbeckia, Briza media*, and *Stipa tenuissima*. In a shady spot, *Anemone x hybrida* can replace other flowers.

YOU WILL NEED

An upcycled box big enough for at least ten plants

A drill with a metal drill bit

Plastic or impermeable liner (thick for maximum insulation) or use bubble wrap with holes cut in it for drainage

Small pottery pieces or small stones

Soil—most types will do, depending on your plant species, but a multipurpose soil mixed with topsoil is fine for most species

Horticultural sand

Grasses of your choice

Flowering plants of your choice

METHOD

1. Drill at least five good-sized (0.8-inch [2-cm] diameter) holes in the bottom of your container for drainage.

2. Spread the liner inside the container for insulation—you don't need to attach it (metal is very hard to attach anything to); the soil will hold it in place once the container is filled. If you prefer, you can apply masking tape to the liner until the soil is in place.

3. Make five big holes in the liner, corresponding with those you've drilled into the bottom of the pot, to allow water to drain away.

4. Place plenty of broken-pot pieces in the bottom of the container; they don't have to cover the whole base, but the more you use, the less chance there is of your container becoming waterlogged. If you don't have enough pottery pieces, some small stones will do the job.

5. Mix the compost with some sand—a few scoops or shovelfuls will do.

6. Fill the container with your soil mix two-thirds of the way up.

7. Arrange the grasses and flowers in the container according to be where you are putting the container (see opposite). Play with the planting arrangement until you are happy—you can always move plants around later if you change your mind.

8. Fill any gaps around the plants' root balls with the remaining soil and then water them in well.

9. Feed the plants a little throughout the growing season with some slow-release fertilizers, but try not to overdo it. Perennials don't need as much food as annual plants.

ARRANGING PLANTS IN A CONTAINER

If the container will be viewed from all directions, you may want to put the tallest plants in the center, but concealing plants behind taller plants so that they're seen only from certain angles can be effective, especially in modern designs. If your container will be set against a wall, put the tallest plants at the back so that all of them are shown off to their full potential. You could also cascade everything down from one corner. In a lot of prairie planting, the plants are arranged in a linear style, which is a nice option—just put all the plants of any one species in a line together.

UPCYCLED WORK BOOTS

🕐 **1 HOUR**

The great thing about outdoor work boots is that they are so large. But what do you do when you are finished with them? They are not fit for use and are unsafe once they get old and worn through, but with all of that space inside, they really lend themselves to being turned into containers.

This project should be planted in the spring so that your bedding plants have time to produce the best displays. When choosing your plants, simply pick your favourite colors. The varieties I have used (see opposite) are easy to find and come in a huge range of colors, so you can change the display every year. If you are not a fan of annuals, then grow perennials instead; just feed the pots every year and change the soil every couple of years. These containers are incredibly versatile and lightweight, allowing you to easily move them around and to swap out the plants to maximise their impact throughout the season.

YOU WILL NEED

A pair (or even a few pairs) of old work boots
Drill (optional)
Pieces of broken pots/pottery
Multipurpose soil
Slow-release fertilizer or granular fertilizer
Dibber (optional)
Annual bedding of your choice—
in plugs in the spring is best (I used marigolds, petunias, *Senecio cineraria*, *Tagetes*, begonias, and geraniums.)

METHOD

1. Make sure there are holes in the bottom of your old boots. If they don't already have them from overuse, drill a few into the rubber sole, being careful of any steel midsoles they may have.
2. Place a few pieces of pottery in the bottom of the boots for drainage.
3. Fill the boots with soil mixed with a little fertilizer. Using a dibber or your finger, make holes in the soil and place a plug plant in each hole. Firm the soil around each plant.
4. Water the finished boots and feed every two weeks with a liquid fertilizer, such as tomato feed, seaweed feed, or comfrey tea (page 57). After the bedding has gone over, collect their seeds (to use next year) on a dry day and compost the plant material.
5. They will flourish in almost any position as long as they get some sun and plenty of food and water. Bedding plants really want to flower, so they will cope with most positions. Do protect them from very high winds, though, so that their tender stems do not snap.

I have used a variety of hues for a bright display, including classics like *Petunia*, *Senecio cineraria*, *Tagetes*, and *Begonia*.

5

WILDLIFE GARDEN IN AN UPCYCLED SUITCASE

🕐 1 HOUR

The best way to create a natural ecosystem in your garden is to make it a haven not only for you, but for the local wildlife, too. Butterflies and bees make your yard feel like a secluded patch of wilderness, and introducing wildlife is also a great way to get kids excited about the great outdoors. Incidentally, insect-friendly plants also tend to be the most floriferous and beautiful. What works for the bees works for us, too.

For something a little different, and much cheaper, than a big container, try using an old suitcase. Used suitcases are easy to find in thrift stores or at garage sales for a fraction of the price you would pay for more traditional containers of the same size. The suitcase will need to be able to withstand some weather, so look for one made of wood or tough leather. It will break down a little over the course of a few years, but this will only add to its vintage look. You will be surprised how well leather wears, even in the great outdoors.

YOU WILL NEED

Old suitcase made from wood or tough leather, deep enough for a 3-liter pot and wide enough for at least six plants

Drill (or utility knife if you're using a leather suitcase or if you don't have a drill)

Washed horticultural sand, plus pea gravel to mulch

Buddleja, Salvia, Sedum, lavender, borage, *Allium, Veronicastrum, Phlox,* mallow, *Hebe, Papaver,* foxglove, or *Campanula*

Soil – not too heavy, including bark or pea gravel

METHOD

1. Drill or cut holes in the bottom of the suitcase to create drainage. Generally speaking, the more the merrier because these plants require a fairly free-draining soil, but you need at least five good-sized holes.

2. Place the suitcase in its final position. If you have a small suitcase, you can move it after planting, but generally, especially with a large container, it is better to plant it in situ.

3. Add a 1–2-inch (2.5–5-cm) -deep layer of washed horticultural and or pea gravel o the bottom of the suitcase and cover with a few inches of soil. This should form a layer on which you can place the plants so that the tops of their root balls come to about 1 inch (2.5 cm) from the rim. This way, you avoid burying your plants too deeply.

4. Place the plants in the suitcase in a pleasing arrangement. The *Buddleja* and *Salvia* (or any other taller plants) should go at the back of your arrangement so they do not block the light for the other plants. The *Sedum* will be lovely at the front, where it can tumble over the edge of the case.

5. Once you are happy, backfill with more soil until the soil level is just below the rim of the suitcase.

6. Dress the soil with a layer of pea gravel to finish it off.

7. Water the container well so that all of the roots are guaranteed to make good contact with the soil.

8. Cut the *Buddleja* back in the early spring so that it can grow nicely through the season. Cut the lavender in spring but do not go into the woody stems. Cut the other plants back in autumn and protect them from the worst of the frost. Every year, give a light feed of compost and top off with mulch, and then repot and replace the soil completely every three to four years.

TIP: This particular arrangement does best when placed in the sun or partial shade because all of these plants require some sunlight. This placement is also a great way to make sure that the insects see the plants!

73

6

WINDOWSILL HERB GARDEN IN A DISPLAY CRATE

🕐 1 HOUR

From a gardener's perspective, herbs are a delight to grow. They need hardly any water, feeding, or root space, which means you can grow them in the smallest spaces with relative success. For the best plants to start with, go to a garden center or grow them from seed (especially basil—nothing ever tastes as good as basil grown from seed). Herbs in a garden center are intended for further growing rather than for instant eating, so I would recommend them over anything you buy from the supermarket.

Another great thing about growing herbs in one pot, particularly if you stick to Mediterranean herbs, such as oregano, thyme, rosemary, sage, and marjoram, which all like dry, free-draining soil (with some moisture) and full sunlight, is that it avoids the pitfall of growing plants together that don't like the same conditions, leading to some dying and others thriving over time.

These kinds of herbs don't need much space for their roots because they grow wild on rocky ground, so you can squeeze this little container onto a windowsill or the smallest patio.

TIP: Put the crate somewhere that's easily accessible when you're cooking or eating. Making it the centerpiece on your outdoor table is effective because it releases its herbal scents while you're eating al fresco and is also handy to pick at, too.

YOU WILL NEED

Old wooden crate that will fit on a windowsill or in the middle of a table
Drill and drill bit
Multipurpose soil
Sand
Herbs of your choice

METHOD

1. Make some holes in the base of your container. Herbs need plenty of drainage, so drill at least two holes per plant, each hole at least 0.4 inch (1 cm) in diameter. The more holes, the better, without upsetting the stability of the pot.
2. Mix the soil with the sand in a ratio of about 50:50 and add most of it to the container.
3. Arrange your herbs in the container, making sure the colors and textures are evenly distributed so all of the purples are not in one area and all of the strappy foliage is not together. Spread similar-looking plants around to create a balanced arrangement.
4. Fill any spaces around the plants with the remaining soil and then water the plants well.
5. This container is low maintenance, though you might find that as you use the herbs, they will become depleted of foliage. In time, you might want to replace any herbs that look a bit ragged. Most Mediterranean herbs need minimal water and food, with the exception of basil and coriander, which both need a little more water.

I've used thyme, rosemary, sage, chives, and golden marjoram.

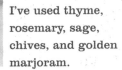

7

BOG GARDEN IN A FARMHOUSE SINK

🕐 **1 HOUR**

Farmhouse sinks are beautiful—so much so that even when sold secondhand, they can be expensive. As an addition to the garden, they are fantastic: clean, crisp, and white, so they look modern, but they are also rustic and sturdy enough to have gravitas and class. They lend themselves best to one of two options: a pond or a bog garden. This is because they have very limited drainage capabilities unless you drill more holes into the base, which would cause their value to depreciate. Turning a farmhouse sink into a bog garden is very simple and adds a touch of mystery to something that is effortlessly stylish.

YOU WILL NEED

Soil

Water-retaining crystals or beads

Farmhouse sink or other nonpermeable container, such as a metal trough or bin or even a big bowl. You will need very few drainage holes—one small hole to get rid of the worst of the moisture should be enough.

Plants—any of those listed at right. Remember that a farmhouse sink is not huge, so stick to three plants maximum. For a modern effect, keep to a single species.

Ligularia dentata 'Othello' or *Ligularia amplexicaulis* 'Britt Marie Crawford'
Rodgersia
Persicaria
Myosotis scopiodes
Rheum palmatum
Gunnera magellanica
Gunnera manicata
Eupatorium
Iris laevigata
Trollius
Geum rivale
Primula japonica
Grasses
Juncus effusus
Carex elata
Ferns
Osmunda regalis
Matteuccia
Athyrium filix-femina
Equisetum

METHOD

1. Mix the soil with water-retaining crystals or beads according to the instructions on the package.
2. Fill the sink with the soil mix, covering the drain with stones or pottery pieces to allow for drainage and to prevent toxic buildup of anaerobic conditions (see opposite).
3. Plant your plants into the soil and water them in.
4. Make sure the plants never dry out by regularly feeling the soil to check if it is moist. If you see any sign of the leaves wilting or becoming curled or crispy, give the pot a good watering. However, make sure that you do not leave the plants sitting in water constantly. Nice and damp is perfect.
5. Cut plants back to the crown (right in the center of the plants), or to a few inches above soil level, once they have died down.
6. Protect the crowns of plants from extreme cold by covering them with horticultural fleece or straw; bog plants usually don't like to be too cold. *Gunnera* can be protected with its own leaves (*Gunnera* has been classified as an invasive plant in the UK and should not be planted anywhere near flowing water there.)

Preventing toxic buildup in soils: When soil is permanently moist, and that moisture has nowhere to go, it becomes waterlogged. After some time, fungi and bacteria will build up in the soil, creating a high sulfur content and making it very hard for plants to extract nutrients. After enough time in these conditions, the soil will become so toxic that the plants can no longer survive.

8

PALLET LIVING WALL

🕐 **AN AFTERNOON**

Pallets are our modern answer to nearly every design conundrum. As I mentioned in the second project, the most arduous part of using a pallet is prying the planks apart and painstakingly removing every nail. In this project, there is no need to do that; you can use the pallet as it is. Just be sure to pick one that looks nice, with no split wood or hanging pieces.

One consideration for a living wall is that it can cause dampness, so it's a good idea to add a plastic backing to your living wall and prepare the wall before you install your feature – a waterproof exterior PVA paint or a special moisture-proof masonry paint does the job. Also, the weight of a watered, plant-filled pallet is quite considerable, so a single-skin wall that goes into your property isn't suitable for this project; neither is a dry stone or crumbly wall. I strongly recommend that if you have any doubts, get a professional to look at the wall you are planning to use before moving forward with this project.

When choosing the position of your living wall, try to avoid a wall that is fully south-facing or north-facing because these positions create challenging conditions for the plants, with either too much heat or too much dampness and cold. An easterly/southeasterly or a westerly/southwesterly position is infinitely better.

YOU WILL NEED

Water-permeable liner
Old pallet (or other living-wall base)
Staple gun or roofing nails and hammer
Sheet of strong plastic
Drill with masonry bit and screwdriver
    attachment
Wall anchors
Screws
Soil
Water-retaining crystals
Plants (preferably including some
    cascading varieties)

Small rooting species, such as strawberries, lettuce, *Galium, Alchemilla*, ferns, succulents, and alpines (mountain plants like *Saxifraga*) work best. For practical gardeners, this is a great opportunity to grow some herbs and vegetables (most annual veggies will survive in semistressed conditions, though they may be more prone to bolting if you are growing leafy vegetables). If you are an ornamental lover, use plants like lavender, creeping rosemary, ivy, sedums and other succulents, trailing lobelia, *Erigeron*, and others. It can be a great idea to create a color scheme for your green wall so that it's actuallyt not so green. Purple is a very effective choice, and there are plenty of purple edibles and ornamentals that grow well in limited space (see page 98).

If you like the linear element of a pallet, you can also make a living wall using the verticals rather than the horizontals. Line the whole pallet interior, leaving a gap at the top. Fill with soil, plant in the gaps, and then leave it flat on the floor until the roots hold the soil in place; otherwise, you will find that things tend to fall out. This version will be much heavier and harder to secure to the wall, though, so you may need assistance.

METHOD

1. Attach the liner behind each horizontal plank of your pallet using the staple gun or roofing nails—double it up if you want to ensure an extra-strong hold. The depth of a pallet plank should be enough to house a plant. The pockets should be deep enough to accommodate the plants' entire root balls. Ideally, the pockets should be no lower than the plant of the pallet, meaning that you will probably need to buy plants that are in 3.5-inch (9-cm) pots or smaller.

2. Affix the strong plastic to the back of the entire pallet with a staple gun or roofing nails to protect your walls from dampness.

3. Drill at least six holes into the wall (two at the bottom, two at the top and two in the middle)—the more attachment points there are, the stronger it will be. (If you are worried about this, you can lean your pallet at an angle against the wall; it does not actually have to be hung on the wall). Insert the wall anchors.

4. Screw your pallet to the wall using screws that fit the wall anchors (make sure you have enough to hang the pallet very securely).

5. Mix your soil with the water-retaining crystals according to the instructions on the packet.

6. Fill each pocket with soil mix. Along each channel of soil, plant your plants, allowing enough room for each of them to grow.

7. If you add a cascading plant every few plants, and stagger them as you move up the height of the pallet, the whole pallet will be engulfed by plants within a few months. This looks much nicer than neat lines.

9

OLD COLANDER HANGING BASKET

⏱ **1 HOUR**

You can make a hanging basket out of a colander, bird cage, wok, cheese grater, or really anything old and metal that you can hang up. These "junk" items make useful containers after they've served their intended purpose. A colander in particular, with its predrilled holes, can become a beautiful hanging basket. It is very free draining and thus ideal for plants that can cope with dry conditions, such as Mediterranean herbs, ivy, succulents, geraniums and other sun lovers. You could also use annual bedding, bought and planted as plugs in the spring, for a brighter, more traditional look.

YOU WILL NEED

Water-permeable liner
Scissors
Old metal or plastic colander
Strong rope or chains
Heavy-duty hooks —they
    must be strong enough to safely
    hold a heavy container complete
    with plants and water (you
    can buy heavy-duty hooks or
    hanging-basket brackets from a
    garden center or online)
Water-retaining crystals
Slow-release fertilizer, such as
    chicken-manure pellets or
    granular feed
Soil
Plants, such as Mediterranean
    herbs, ivy, succulents, geraniums;
    I've used: margerites, *Senecio
    cineraria,* bronze fennel and ivy

Cascading species, such as trailing *Pelargonium*, ivy, *Aubretia*, *Lobelia*, *Lampranthus*, *Sedum*, or *Erigeron* are great in baskets that are hung high up because they bring the flowers or foliage down to eye level, which means you're looking at the plants themselves rather than the base of the pot.

METHOD

1. Cut the liner so that it fits in the colander exactly and attach the rope or chains to it.

2. Screw the hooks into the ceiling or wall (or whatever you're hanging your colander from)—one per hanging basket. Make sure that the hooks are secure and strong enough to hold the weight of the colander plus plants, compost, and, most importantly, water (which is always the heaviest component of a planter).

3. Mix the soil with the water-retaining crystals and fertilizer according to the instructions on the package.

4. Place a little soil in the bottom of the colander and then arrange your plants. Remember that unless the basket is in the center of the garden or right in front of a window, you might only ever see it from three sides, so make sure that your design takes this into account.

5. Backfill any gaps around the roots of the plants with the remaining soil, hang the colander from the hook, and water it well. It is always best to water in situ because the hanging basket will be considerably heavier and harder to hang once it's watered.

6. Feed throughout the summer with a slow-release fertilizer. Add liquid feed to the water when the plants need an extra boost.

10

RAISED BED MADE FROM RAILROAD TIES

🕐 **A WEEKEND**

Raised beds are a great way to grow and, depending on their size, you can grow a very wide range of species. Railroad ties are ideal for raised beds, but they are literally not to be taken lightly! If you have a bad back, you may want to get some help with this project. But the great thing about railroad ties is that once they are in place, they are heavy enough that attaching them at the corners provides enough support. This is a big project but well worth the effort for the amount of growing space it provides, and these raised beds look great—modern but naturalistic. You can make them sleek or a little rough around the edges, depending on how geometric you make your design. I have made two rectangles: one filled with vegetables and the other with wildflowers. I ordered my railroad ties from a lumber merchant at full lengths and precut half-lengths. Cutting these is a professional job, so unless you are fully trained, leave it to the professionals.

YOU WILL NEED

Spade

Gloves, goggles, and steel-toe boots
  Three, six, or nine pressure-treated
  railroad ties, depending how tall you
  want your raised bed

Four wood battens (2 x 2 or 3 x 3 inches
  [5 x 5 or 7.5 x 7.5 cm])

Drill and 1-inch (2.5-cm) wood drill bit

Screwdriver

Long screws or bolts, two per tie

Dowel with 1-inch (2.5-cm) diameter

Wood glue

Mallet

Staple gun

Waterproof liner

Topsoil, about 70 cubic feet (2 cubic
  meters) per rectangle

Compost—you can often find garden-
  waste compost through local garden
  clubs, or you can make it yourself
  (see page 53)

Well-rotted manure (for vegetables only)

Plants—wildflower plug plants, such as
  poppies, cornflowers, and yarrow,
  or vegetable plugs such as kale,
  cabbage, lettuce, climbing green
  beans, tomatoes, beets, and the like.
  I'd designate half of the bed for one
  plant family and the other half for
  another to allow easy crop rotation
  (see page 157).

TIP: You can often get topsoil from local housing developments where they are clearing a lot of it to build new foundations. And if you have already built your beds, they may even fill them for you, saving you hours of carting soil.

METHOD

1. Choose where you want the bed to go—once built, a raised bed is almost impossible to move. Level the ground because any uneven surfaces will make your structure less sturdy and potentially wobbly. The easiest way to do this is to dig with a spade, but don't dig too deeply. If there is a real slope, you may want to create some terracing. The finished result should be a strong, firm surface that can hold the weight of a raised bed. You can create a level base with a concrete foundation, but this will narrow your planting options because the plants' roots won't be able to go deeper than the depth of the bed.

2. Wearing your protective equiepment, lay out your railroad ties; you may want to enlist some helpers for this step

3. With someone holding the railroad ties in place, screw the battens of wood to the inside corners using some hefty bolts or screws. For each corner, you should have at least two screws per tie on each side of the batten so that the corner is held securely. This will prevent the sleepers from moving when you finally attach them and give extra support when they're finished.

4. Drill two holes (about 1 inch [2.5 cm]) into the uncut end of each outer corner with the drill bit.

5. Drill a pilot hole into the wood starting from inside this 1-inch (2.5-cm) hole.

6. Screw in the heavy-duty bolts so that they sit tight with the surface at the back of the 1-inch (2.5-cm) hole and make sure they go well into the attaching railroad tie.

7. Cut a length of dowel that's a little longer than 1 inch (about 3 cm) and cover it with a layer of wood glue. Using the mallet, hammer it into the hole so that it sits flush against the sleeper or just proud of it, if you like a more rustic look.

8. Using the staple gun, attach the liner to the inside of the tie walls, but not along the ground because this would prevent natural drainage.

9. Fill the beds with the compost, topsoil and manure if you are growing vegetables. The majority of the blend should be topsoil, with a few inches' depth of compost and a few inches' depth of manure. Fork it all so that it is nicely mixed.

10. Plant in the spring. Wildflowers need watering in and then regular watering. Vegetables need regular watering and feeding with an organic fertilizer either in liquid form, such as seaweed or comfrey tea, or as granular pellets, such as bonemeal or chicken-manure pellets.

11. In the autumn, cut back your wildflowers; once the seeds have formed, scatter them on the ground for the following year. Keep a few aside to sow in spring and fill in any gaps.

12. Once you have harvested your vegetables, either grow a green manure in the bed during winter or mulch the bed with seasoned farmyard manure to be ready for next year's crops.

GROWING VEGGIES IN RAISED BEDS

In terms of vegetables, the world is your oyster, from brassicas like cabbage, lettuce, and kale to peas and other legumes, as well as fruiting crops such as tomatoes and peppers, nasturtiums, corn (especially effective if planted in a row to separate other plant families), and many more. The only thing you need to remember is that you must rotate the crops every year (see page 157). Also, you may struggle to grow potatoes because they need soil to be mounded up around their growing stems, so they grow better in standard containers.

11

HEDGE IN A POT

🕐 **1 HOUR**

You may not have an outdoor area that requires a huge beech hedge à la Louis XIV and his gardens at Versailles, but even in the humblest of spaces, a little privacy goes a long way. Perhaps you want to eat outside without your neighbors judging your cooking skills, or you want to be more scantily clad in warm weather. Whatever your reasons for privacy, a hedge is a great way to achieve it. If you have a small yard, you can plant that hedge in the ground, but if you really don't have much space, such as on a roof terrace, on a balcony, or in a paved courtyard, a potted hedge is an excellent option. It can also serve as a useful method of division within your garden. Adding height always makes for a more interesting design that plays tricks on the eye, so you could plant a hedge to divide your outdoor space and create private escapes in hidden corners, or to hide eyesores like trampolines and swings from the more adult areas of the yard. (You could also achieve this simply with a row of pots.)

YOU WILL NEED

A trough or several similar-sized pots arranged in a line (you need an absolute minimum of three to achieve the desired effect)

Hedging plants, such as beech, *Griselinia* for a coastal spot, hornbeam, box or yew if you want evergreens, cherry laurel or bamboo, cherry for something productive (or, similarly, an espaliered apple for a flat, attractive, and productive hedge), alder, hazel, or something trained (pleached) for a taller or even two-tier hedge. But anything will do, including lavender, rosemary, and *Phormium*, especially in a tall pot.

Topsoil or multipurpose soil

Stakes and string (optional)

METHOD

1. Move the trough or containers into position before you start planting to make sure everything is in the right place; otherwise, they will be heavy and difficult to move once planted, particularly in the case of the trough.
2. Put a thin layer of soil in the bottom of the container(s).
3. Lay out your hedging plants root ball to root ball or so that the foliage knits together at the top and you cannot see through it. If you are using espaliered apples or trained specimens, leave a large gap between the root balls so that the edges of the branches just or almost touch.
4. Backfill around the plants and into any spaces with the remaining soil. Pat down the soil with your hands.
5. You may want to attach a stake or frame for additional support if the area is exposed to wind—on a roof terrace or balcony, for example. Push a stake or cane into the soil and tie the hedge plant to it, using string. In severely windy spots, you may want to stake at a 45-degree angle into the prevailing wind, or attach your plants using string to a balustrade, fence, or trellis.
6. Water well. Feed with a slow-release fertilizer once a year or mulch with compost in the winter.
7. Refresh the soil or repot either every few years or f the leaves begin to lose their luster, the plants do not flower as vigorously or look a little cramped, or the leaves begin to discolor; all of these signs indicate a lack of nutrients.

TIP: It's best to do this project in autumn or winter when you can buy bare-root shrubs and trees for far less than container-grown ones will cost in the spring or summer.

x

PROJECTS

12

NEVER THROW AWAY A CAN AGAIN!

🕐 1 HOUR

There is a lot of visual worth and versatility in a tin can. Andy Warhol recognized it, and gardeners are recognizing it, too. Cans are great because they are so changeable. They start off with glossy labels, and they eventually age and begin to oxidize and rust. They come in varying sizes, too, and are usually filled with delicious food, so you have the best of both worlds—you can eat the can's contents then grow plants in the receptacle. And if you're food obsessed like me, you can grow more food in it in the form of vegetables or herbs. Tin cans are also fairly lightweight compared to a lot of containers, which means you can arrange them in many ingenious ways, such as by screwing them to the wall or upright on a balcony or pergola.

YOU WILL NEED

Tin cans—as many as you have, and you can add to your collection as time goes on. They don't all have to be the same size—the more varied, the better!

Drill

Varnish and paintbrush

Screws, if needed

Sand or pea gravel for drainage

Water-retaining crystals

Soil

Plants—anything small will lend itself to this project because there will be limited root space. Strawberries, lettuces, and herbs are the best edibles, while succulents, annuals, mosses, and alpines make the best ornamentals.

METHOD

1. Drill drainage holes in the bottom of your cans. One hole per can is OK if you use enough gravel, but I suggest three (more for large cans) to be on the safe side.

2. Varnish the inside of the can; a tin can is actually made from steel and coated with tin or aluminium, so the coating will eventually wear away to expose the steel beneath. The coating gets into the soil, and the rusting steel will do the same. This is not good for the plants because increased heavy metals in the soil lead to a change in pH and affect the plants' ability to soak up nutrients. These compounds in the soil are also very harmful to humans if eaten, so a layer of varnish is especially important if you are planning to grow edibles.

3. Wait for the varnish to dry; this will take from twelve to forty-eight hours. If in doubt, wait longer; tacky varnish could mean that the soil sticks to the can, which would look dreadful and be hard to get off.

4. Using a drill, make a hole in the back of the can and then screw it onto a wall or post. The positioning of the tins dictates what you can grow, so place alpines in bright, exposed locations and mosses or ferns in shady corners. If it's a dry spot, choose succulents.

5. Mix the sand or pea gravel and the soil together, making a 50:50 mix, and then add the water-retaining crystals according to the package's instructions. Add a layer of the mixture to the bottom of the tin.

6. Place the plants in the tin. Backfill around the roots with the remaining soil mix until the pots are full. Water well.

7. Succulents must come indoors during wet winters. For ferns, you may need to replenish the soil every few years or apply mulch of fresh compost every year. Cut any dead, dying, or diseased material off your plants as soon as you see it.

13

SUCCULENT PICTURE FRAME

🕐 **AN AFTERNOON**

As a gardener, you have to do absolutely nothing in order to successfully grow succulents. They need minimal watering; in a temperate climate, they're more likely to be killed off from excessive water than from drought. They need hardly any root space, and they propagate with absolutely no effort (see the tip on page 95). This extraordinary talent for survival makes them incredibly versatile. You can grow succulents in the smallest of spaces (stuffed into a hollowed-out cork) or en masse in a huge area. They make great table centerpieces because they never get too tall and they look lovely cascading from any upcycled receptacle: tea pots, tin cans, displays of tiny pots, the cracks in gnarled wood, and the list goes on.

There are the traditional rosette forms that have become very popular and come in all colors, textures, and sizes—hairy, fluffy, chalky white, green, purple, black, red, and so on—but they can be susceptible to damping off in the autumn and over winter. If you live somewhere with a colder, wetter climate, there are many traditional succulents, such as sedums, that are more tolerant of a little rain and cold. For some people (myself included) who live by the sea, succulents like *Lampranthus* (or, as people where I live affectionately know it, "pig face") are some of the only reliable plants that grow in the salty conditions.

For this project, I am making a picture frame crammed full of succulents to hang on the wall. The finished product will fit into a small space, will need minimal water, and could even be complemented by some battery-powered or solar lighting for maximum effect.

YOU WILL NEED

An old picture frame with a deep recess of about 2 inches (5 cm)

Thin plywood and small dowels

Screws

Drill

Chicken wire or mesh

Soil

Horticultural sand

Dibber

An array of succulents, some hanging (like *Sedum rupestre*, *Sedum spathulifolium*, or *Crassula multicava*) and some rosettes (like *Sempervivum tectorum*, *S. arachnoideum* [which means "like spiderwebs"), *S. calcareum*, *Echeveria glauca*, *E. agavoides* 'Black Prince,' or *Sedum* x *rubrotinctum*

METHOD

1. If the picture frame has a glass front, remove the glass and dispose of it safely.
2. Make a box to fit on the back of the picture frame using the plywood screwed together with the dowels.
3. Where the glass would normally go, attach the chicken wire or mesh.
4. Secure the box to the back of the picture frame.
5. Drill holes for drainage in the bottom of the picture frame; you need a lot of holes because succulents need very good drainage.
6. Mix the soil with plenty of sand. Pour the soil into the picture-frame box.
7. Break off succulent plants into individual plugs. Poke holes between each segment of the wire mesh and put a succulent plant into each hole. Water well.
8. Wait for a few weeks before hanging the picture frame to allow the succulents to establish themselves; otherwise, you run the risk of the plants falling out.

TIP: You will see the plants start to produce small babies all over their foliage; when that happens, break them off and stick each one in a little pot of soil so that they'll grow into bigger plants that can then be added to container displays.

14

MAGNETIC POT DISPLAYS

🕐 **1 HOUR**

We all have dead space in our yards that hardly get used, but what if you could use these traditionally useless areas for growing? Believe it or not, there is a way.

Magnetic pots are the future. We may not all have metal spaces that are suitable for sticking pots to, but look a little closer—I bet you have more metallic surfaces than you think. Uprights on a balcony, railings, a backsplash for your grill, the edges of water features, or garden furniture? Even if you don't have these spaces, metal panels are easy to find and attach to most surfaces. And with a huge range of magnetic pots available (or, for the adventurous, strong magnets, allowing you to make your own) there is a lot of fun to be had and a lot of practical solutions to be found with magnetic containers.

Magnetic pots do tend to be rather small, though, so don't use plants that have very deep roots or need a lot of space. Plants like strawberries work really well. Also, depending where your metallic surfaces are, your pots will either be mostly in the shade or mostly in the sun. Under the balcony, where mine are, they are in shade, so I am using an *Asplenium* (hart's-tongue fern) and an *Epimedium*, both of which love shady conditions. For a sunny spot, plants like *Erigeron* or any number of herbs, including thyme, chamomile, lavender, curry plants, and many more, are good. Alternatively, alpines are great options for a sunny, exposed position. Naturally mountain dwellers, these plants can cope with very restricted root space, extreme brightness, and harsh wind. *Raoulia*, *Lewisia*, *Lithodora*, and *Veronica* are some particularly nice examples.

YOU WILL NEED

Plants of your choice—for edibles, strawberries and other shallow rooters will be best; for ornamentals, there is a wider choice, but ferns and foliage-heavy plants like ivy work really well
Magnetic container
Multipurpose soil
Water-retaining crystals
A metal area, such as a beam or an entire wall, or metal sheets that can be attached to a wall

METHOD

1. Place the plants in the pot.
2. Combine the soil with the water-retaining crystals according to the instructions on the package.
3. Put the soil mix around the root balls of the plants. Most of the magnetic pots you can buy come without holes so that water doesn't drip down the fridge and ruin your floors, so they often incorporate an internal element that raises the plant up off the base to prevent them from sitting in water.
4. Water well and then stick the pots to your metal surface.
5. Water regularly, keeping the soil permanently moist but never wet.

TIP: If you really want to invest in magnetic pots, and you have a large metal space—maybe the side of a corrugated metal shed—a mass of magnetic pots can create a stunning living wall.

15

LIVING WALL
🕐 A WEEKEND

Living walls are becoming ever more popular as a solution to the problem of creating green areas in our yards at a time when outdoor space is increasingly at a premium. They can also reduce noise pollution and can actually lower our energy bills by helping insulate our homes from the outside.

Creating a living wall is incredibly easy; the only requirement is that you use plants that can cope with restricted root space. If you buy these plants as very small specimens, they can be very cheap.

YOU WILL NEED

Vertical planter made out of water-permeable liner or any other material. There are fabric-pocket planters or more robust systems in which soil bags slide into metal hangers. Liner pockets are the cheapest option.

Wood for the frame—cheap wood will do; it needs to be strong, but it won't be seen

Wall anchors

Screws

Sheet of strong plastic the same size as your planter and frame

Staple gun

Sheet of thick, water-retaining fabric, such as felt

Irrigation system (optional but recommended)

Soil

Water-retaining crystals

Hooks

Plants to put in the pouches (see the list on page 80 for the Pallet Living Wall project). Any plant with a shallow root system can cope here, whether edible or ornamental.

METHOD

1. Do this project with plugs in the spring. Measure the area you want to turn into a living wall. If you want to use an existing wall, choose a strong surface, preferably one that has been waterproofed with exterior PVA or moisture-proof masonry paint. It should also be strong enough to carry some weight and ideally should not be north- or south-facing, but a happy medium for optimal growing conditions. A freestanding living wall can go in front of any structure because it will not put any strain on it.

2. Build a frame, the same size as the hanging material you have made or bought, out of wood. This frame needs to be square or rectangular, depending on the size of the living wall, and supported by horizontal and vertical struts to maximize its strength. Drill it together with wood screws.

3. Attach this frame to the wall using wall anchors and screws. You must attach it very securely because it will hold up the whole structure, which will be quite heavy when finished.

4. Affix the plastic sheet to the frame with a staple gun. You don't want any dampness getting into your wall because it could damage your property. Attach the water-retaining fabric over the plastic.

5. Install any irrigation systems (see Tip).

6. Attach the liner with pockets or a metal hanger to this whole structure, using screws or very strong staples.

7. Place the plants into the pockets making sure you are evenly distributing textures and colours. If it is well balanced, it will grow nicely. Alternatively, you might want to separate the colors into distinct groups with brighter plants in one area and softer plants in another.

8. Mix the soil with water-retaining crystals according to the instructions on the package and then add the compost to any gaps in the pockets. Water well.

9. Feed throughout the growing season with liquid fertilizer; water regularly.

TIP: Unless you are very diligent about watering, or your green wall is in a rainy spot, it's worth investing in an **irrigation system**. They are easy to find and relatively inexpensive. You can also get solar-powered options or attach them to rain barrels to reduce your water bills.

16

CONTAINERS FOR A ROOF TERRACE

⏱ **AN AFTERNOON**

Every element that plants endure on the ground is experienced tenfold by those that are positioned higher up—on balconies or terraces, in hanging baskets or rooftop gardens—because wind is stronger the higher up you go, UV rays are more intense, and life is generally tougher. In high UV and high winds, plants dry out very quickly, so when planning a roof terrace it is important to pick species that can cope with such intense conditions (see opposite). If in doubt, think "mountainside." If you choose something that you recognize from a mountain or think would be at home on a mountain, from the smallest alpine species to the largest conifer, you're heading in the right direction.

There is one other, obvious, thing to consider, and that is your pots. In high winds, containers have an annoying habit of falling over, so it is best to make or buy very sturdy pots or, even better, to build the pots into the garden itself by integrating raised beds or, at the very least, screwing down any wooden pots. At the same time, be careful that you do not overload your roof with very heavy pots. To avoid this, fill the bottom half of the pots with polystyrene to minimize the weight and don't put more pots on the roof than can be supported. If in doubt, go for lighter pots and make provisions for high winds, such as screwing the pots down.

YOU WILL NEED

Water-retaining crystals
Soil
Plants (see opposite)
Stakes and string or rubber plant ties (optional)

METHOD

1. Add water-retaining crystals to your soil according to the instructions on the package.
2. Plant your plants in raised beds or pots.
3. Stake the stems of the plants to no higher than a third of their height tif they looks vulnerable to the wind. To do so, stick a stake in the soil, preferably at a 45-degree angle, facing into the prevailing wind. Tie the plant to the stake using string or a rubber tie.
4. Water regularly at the roots rather than the foliage because the sun will bake any sitting water and cause the leaves to scorch.
5. It may be worth installing an irrigation system in exposed locations because the winds can dry out your plants. This is especially useful if you have a lot of pots; otherwise, a rain barrel and watering can will do the job.
6. Regularly sweep and remove snapped stems with clean pruning shears. Keep plants well watered and feed them with a mulch of composted manure, composted leaves or soil in the winter. Feed with a granular feed such as bonemeal during the summer.

PERFECT PLANTS FOR ALTITUDE

If the label on the plant isn't clear as to whether or not it will survive tougher, more exposed conditions, look for a few of these telltale signs, which will point you to just the right plant.

Adaptations for high UV

Silver foliage

Chalky substance on leaves

White hairs on leaves

Low-lying foliage

Rosette formation of leaves

Bright flowers (bonus)

Little leaves

Big flowers

Adaptations for high wind

Flexible stems

Tough leaves or needles

Small foliage

Quick to regenerate after
    losing limbs

Thick, robust trunks

17

HOMEMADE NEWSPAPER POTS

🕐 **1 HOUR**

Paper pots offer an alternative to the compostable pots available from garden centers for growing plants from seed. An essential part of seed growing is the pricking-out stage once the seedlings are big enough to go into more nutrient-rich soil and bigger pots. Making your own paper pots is a good green option; you can use old newspapers and then recycle or compost them once they're too soggy to use. If you want something a little more decorative, use wrapping paper; if you want to keep plants indoors, you can grow plants like cacti in paper bags because they need hardly any water.

YOU WILL NEED

Paper of your choice
Tube from toilet paper, paper towels, or a poster—even a paper cup will do
Sand
Soil—low nutrient for seeds and cuttings
Seedlings, seeds, cuttings, or plants of your choice. This is also a great way of growing seedlings and cuttings for other container projects, like a hanging basket, living wall, or bedding display

METHOD

1. Roll the paper around the tube or cup to cover; two layers of thickness will do, but for a plant that will stay in the paper pot a little longer, like a cutting, make more layers.
2. Fold the paper underneath at just one end.
3. Make firm folds so that the paper stays in place and dip the bottom of the tube in water so that it holds its shape.
4. Combine the sand and soil (the ratio of the mix will depend on what plants you are growing) and then fill the tubes with the mix.
5. Either sow seeds into each tube, prick out seedlings into them, or put in one cutting per pot. Water well.
6. When the pot becomes too soggy, either peel away the paper and transplant the plant, or plant the paper pot straight into the ground with the plant still in it. It will break down and eventually supply some compost to the soil.

Paper pots are best used as greenhouse or windowsill pots because excessive rain makes them very soggy very quickly. In a greenhouse, the pots last long enough to grow seedlings and harden them off, after which you can even plant the seedlings, in their pots, straight into the ground.

← **To take cuttings:**

- Select healthy, nonflowering shoots from the plant.

- Cut these shoots off just above a node (leaf joint).

- Trim the cut sprig to just under a leaf joint.

- Remove all lower foliage, just leaving the tops.

- Dib a hole in the soil and stick in the cutting.

- Water.

18

CONCRETE JUNGLE

🕐 **A WEEKEND**

Concrete is immensely versatile. Although wet concrete or cement is toxic to plants, it poses no problem when fully hardened. You can make your own concrete container in any shape or size.

I put a *Phormium* in my concrete container because the beautiful, sword-like leaves give a sleek edge to the industrial pot. This container is great for any plant that has earned notoriety, as many exotic, slightly "invasives" have; for example, running bamboo can be beautiful, but it does tend to take over, and if left unchecked, *Phormium* will become enormous! One thing that stops this is concrete. So what better marriage than your homemade concrete container and your prized *Phormium* or bamboo, brought together in a way that both complements and contains them?

YOU WILL NEED

Drop cloth
Garbage can (that you don't
     mind getting messy)
Old, thick blanket
Very runny concrete mix of 3:1
     sand and cement
Bucket to mix cement in
Masonry paint and paintbrush (optional)
Exotic-looking plant of your choice
Decorative stone for container (see Tip)

METHOD

1. Lay the drop cloth on the floor with the upturned garbage can on top of it. Do this in an area of your yard that you don't mind getting messy, and wear old clothes! You should do this project in an area that is protected from the elements, or pick a dry day when the forecast is rain free for at least twenty-four hours.

2. Dip the blanket in the runny concrete mix until it is thickly covered and then drape it over the upturned garbage can. Let it dry for a minimum of twenty-four hours but preferably a few days.

3. Once the blanket is fully hardened, remove it from the garbage can and turn it over; it should now resemble a plant pot. At this stage, you can paint the pot, if you like, using masonry paint. Move the pot to its final position because it will be very heavy when filled with soil and a plant. Bamboo and Phormium are not fussy and can grow nearly anywhere you like, preferably with a little shade

Phormium tenax comes in a gorgeous range of different colors.

during the day and the chance to catch raindrops because they like to be moist.

4. Place your plant, still in its plastic pot, into the concrete container. There are no drainage holes in the concrete container, so you can't plant straight into it; otherwise, the roots will rot. Making a hole in the base could potentially let bamboo runners (if that's what you're planting) escape into the garden, which is precisely what you are trying to prevent!

5. Cover the soil surface in the plastic pot with decorative pebbles to dress up the feature.

6. Water fairly regularly so that the pot never fully dries out.

TIP: Think about the color of pebble that you use. If you painted your container, choose pebbles that offset that color nicely; if not, use a gray or pale-colored stone to harmonize with your concrete container.

19

POND IN A METAL TROUGH

🕐 **AN AFTERNOON**

We all love ponds, including the small creatures and birds that visit your garden and yard. However, there are a few things to consider about having a pond. A pond can be thought of as quite traditional and (dare I say) a bit messy, as well as a lot of work to build, requiring considerable outdoor space. But it is possible to have a small container pond (pot-sized!) in any corner of the yard. And if you get your container right, it can be anything but traditional. You could make one using glass for a contemporary look that is also perfect for helping educate young children about different habitats and insects. Here, though, I have chosen an old animal-feed trough for its rustic yet geometric charm— industrial chic meets cottage garden.

YOU WILL NEED

Fully watertight container
Garden hose
Oxygenating plants like hornwort, spiked water milfoil, or water violet
Gravel or stones
Water-loving plants (see overleaf)—you will find a wide selection at a nursery that specializes in aquatic plants
Upturned pots and stones to maintain proper depth and allow wildlife access into and out of the pond

METHOD

1. Clean the container, preferably with plain rainwater; if not, use tap water. Do not use strong chemicals because they will potentially contaminate the water and make it a hostile environment for plants.

2. Fill the container with water from a rain barrel. If you are using tap water, you will need to let it sit for a few weeks before adding any fish.

3. Add oxygenating plants, which will stay submerged near the bottom.

4. Place water lilies (dwarf varieties) at the bottom of the container.

5. Place gravel or stones on the soil surrounding your aquatic plants in their pots to weigh them down.

6. Place upturned flowerpots or rocks in the water to prop up the plants you will be putting in the water.

7. On top of these, place your aquatic plants, still in their pots and weighed down with gravel or stones.

8. Move the pots around until you are happy with their arrangement.

I am using *Iris laevigata*, *Nymphaea pygmaea* (dwarf water lily), and *Equisetum fluviatile*. (Water lilies need to be dwarf varieties, or they will quickly take over.)

GUTTER STRAWBERRIES ⏱ 1 HOUR

The beauty of growing strawberries in a metal gutter is that it is a mutually beneficial relationship: as well as looking fantastic and fitting almost anywhere (a wall, a table edge, along the roof of your house or shed), the strawberries actually grow better for it and taste delicious because hanging fruits keep slugs and snails at bay. The only thing you need to do to ensure the best fruit is feed and water the plants regularly in early summer.

YOU WILL NEED

Old (or new) metal gutters of
    the required length to fit your space
Drill and screws
Gutter clips/brackets to install them
Wall anchors, if they're going into a brick wall
Soil
Water-retaining crystals
Strawberry plants to fill the gutters—as
    a rough guide, you'll need a plant
    approximately every 6 inches (15 cm).

METHOD

1. Drill holes in the gutters at regular 4-inch (10-cm) intervals.
2. Attach the gutters to the wall with screws or, if you have gutter clips or brackets, attach them to the wall first before hanging the gutter. It is helpful to put them out of reach of slugs and snails, and in a spot where they will get plenty of sunshine and some rain, so you won't have to water as often.
3. Mix the compost with the water-retaining crystals according to the instructions on the package.
4. Place the strawberry plants in the gutter, 6 inches (15 cm) apart. Fill any gaps around the plants with soil mix and water the plants well.
5. Water regularly. In wet weather, the rain should do the work for you, but remember that shallow roots dry out quickly, so water every day when it's hot and dry.
6. Feed with a high-potassium feed like liquid tomato feed, liquid seaweed fertilizer, or comfrey tea in early summer to get the best fruit.

GRASS HEDGE IN A SCAFFOLD-PLANK TROUGH

🕐 **AN AFTERNOON**

Scaffold planks are good quality and very tough, so any projects you create with them will last a long time. Because they are long, slender planks, they lend themselves to being turned into a trough by simply screwing the planks together.

Grasses are a fantastic option for these troughs. They are known as "transparent plants" because you can see light through them, yet they offer privacy and seclusion. There is a wide range of grasses available in different heights and shapes. Some are erect and round, while others hang and drape in elegant curves; some are 8 feet (2.5 m) tall, while others are shorter than 1 foot (30.5 cm). They also come in different colors, from purples to whites, silver-blues, and deepest greens, offering all kinds of variegation.

YOU WILL NEED

Gloves and goggles
Claw hammer (optional)
Three scaffold planks. They come in
    lengths of 6, 8, 10, and 12 feet and
    should be a standard width and depth.
Sandpaper
Drill with drill bit
Screws
Staple gun
Water-permeable liner
Multipurpose soil with some sand mixed in
Grasses of your choice—I used
    Pennisetum macrourum, but
    *Miscanthus sinesnsis, Panicum
    virgatum* 'Heavy Metal,' *Calamagrostis
    acutiflora* 'Karl Foerster,' or *Stipa
    tenuissima* would all work well.

METHOD

1. Remove the metal from the end of each planks with a claw hammer, unless you like them as a feature, in which case, leave them on.
2. Cut a length of 7 inches (178 mm) off two of the planks. These cut pieces will form the end pieces for your trough.
3. Cut your planks to the required length (the space you have for the trough). If you cut them carefully, you may have long enough boards to make two troughs and form a corner. If you want them as long as possible, remove 7 inches (178 mm) from the end of the third plank to give the maximum length per trough.
4. Sand the ends with sandpaper to remove any splinters and to guarantee a good finish.
5. Drill 0.8-inch (2-cm) -diameter holes into one of the three planks at a distance of about 8 inches (20 cm) apart. This will provide drainage.
6. Place the plank with the holes in it on the ground; this is the base of your trough.
7. In front of that board, place another plank, standing on its side, at 90 degrees from the base plank, to form the front. Make sure the plank is on the ground, not on top of the base plank, to give a neater finish.
8. Screw the plank onto the base along the front edge. You may need to brace it so that the screws go easily into the wood. Repeat with the back plank.
9. You should now have a U-shaped profile. Slot your two end pieces of wood into their final positions, which will turn your U-shape into a square.

TIP: For something really special, consider growing an annual edible-grass trough in the form of barley, wheat, rice, oats, or, for the most impact, a statuesque corn hedge, which will give you 8 feet (about 2.5 m) of growth in a year and produce delicious cobs. Better for the wildlife and better for you!

10. Screw the end pieces to the front plank and back plank with approximately four screws per side. Make sure the screws are in a straight line for a neat finish.

11. Staple the liner to the inside of the container.

12. Put a 1.5-inch (3–4-cm) layer of the soil mix along the bottom of the trough.

13. Place your grasses in the trough and move them around until you are happy with the effect. As grasses can be quite ephemeral, especially when they are young, arrange them fairly close together and stagger them slightly to create a thicker look. You can always thin them out after a few years if the plants get too crowded.

14. Using the remaining soil, fill in any gaps around the roots of the plants and then water.

15. Keep moist but not wet. You shouldn't need to water too regularly because the rain will do it for you, but there will be a lot of roots that will use up water quickly. If it doesn't rain for a few days, feel the soil. If it is dry to the touch, give the plants some water.

16. Feed throughout the growing season with slow-release or granular fertilizer, but don't overdo it; grasses will cope with little feeding. If you are growing corn (see Tip), you will need to feed it more regularly if you want healthy cobs.

22

BRICK RAISED BED FOR FERNS

🕐 **A WEEKEND**

Regardless of how much space you have, you should include a few ferns somewhere in your garden or yard. They tend to prefer high moisture levels and positions on the shady side, though there are certain species that prefer dry, sunny spots. Some are evergreen, while others die back in winter and flourish again in spring, when they unfurl beautiful fronds. They all spore during the first stage of reproduction, which means they have the added interest of spore-producing fronds in the latter part of the season. The famous tree fern (*Dicksonia antarctica*) is stately and jungle-like; one of my personal favorites, the hart's-tongue fern (*Asplenium scolopendrium*) is fairy-like and mysterious.

You can use pots of any kind to house your ferns, but bricks are a favorite building material for good reason: they are relatively cheap and easy to use. If you are rendering your wall, this project will be even cheaper if you use concrete blocks rather than fired bricks. Once the mortar has hardened, a brick wall of any kind is an incredibly strong structure, which is important because soil and compost are heavy, especially when wet. Ferns combine beautifully with brick beds because, despite their prehistoric origins, they have a minimalist, modern look and their fronds and delicately cut leaves provide a gentleness and softness that seem to transcend fashion and trends.

YOU WILL NEED

Trowel or spade

Pointing cement trowel

Coarse builder's sand/aggregate

Vibratory plate compacter (optional)

Cement

Fine sand

Plasticizer (liquid dish detergent will do)

Bricks—either classic red or yellow bricks, cinder blocks, or concrete blocks. Concrete is the cheapest option because you will need fewer of them than smaller bricks, but because they are thinner, you need more compost and soil to fill your beds. If you are not rendering your wall, bricks look vastly superior.

Level

Rubber mallet

Render mix

Plastering trowel

Masonry paint and paintbrush

Topsoil

Compost

Gravel or sand for soil (optional)

Ferns (see opposite)

METHOD

1. Find or create an area of level ground in your yard and then dig a trench about 4 inches (10 cm) deep and the same width as your wall will be.

2. Fill the trench with aggregate and compact it thoroughly. You might want to rent a plate compactor because this layer needs to be very firm because to form the foundation for your wall. If you have concrete on the ground, or extremely compacted soil, you may be able to skip this step. If you are unsure, seek professional advice.

3. Using a ratio of 3:1 fine sand to cement, mix your mortar. Add water until it is the consistency of ice cream—it needs to be soft enough to move and mold but solid enough not to lose its shape. Add plasticizer (just a little squeeze per bucketload of cement) and mix in thoroughly.

4. Add mortar to the bricks as you place them in a neat pattern, ensuring that they all adhere together nicely. When laying bricks on the row below, always apply mortar on the existing wall and the brick end that points forward so that the next brick fits snugly into an L-shaped bed of mortar and sticks well.

5. After you lay each brick, place the level on top of it and the adjoining brick, banging the top of the level with a rubber mallet until the new brick sits level.

6. Let the mortar dry for at least twenty-four hours or a few days of nice weather to ensure full dryness, if possible, before rendering the outer layer.

7. Using your render mix according to the instructions on the package, smooth on the render from the bottom upwith your plastering trowel, filling in any gaps and scraping to a smooth finish. You can leave a little texture if you'd like; if not, regularly rinse your trowel between applications and run it over the wall until you are happy with the result. (You can skip these steps by hiring a professional to build and render your wall.)

8. Paint the rendered wall once the render has dried. (Some renders come in precolored mixes, so you won't need to paint.) Drying times vary according to the product you use; check the package for drying instructions. In most cases, you will need to wait at least two or three dry days for your render to dry, but it's better to wait longer if possible.

9. Fill the raised bed with a mixture of topsoil and compost at a ratio of 50:50, concentrating more compost in the top 12 inches (30 cm) of the bed. Ferns grow naturally under trees, so a homemade leaf compost is a cheap and effective growing medium for them. If you built your raised bed on a concrete base, I strongly recommend adding a healthy layer of gravel (about 4 inches [10 cm]) to the bottom of the bed and mix gravel or sand into the compost mix in the rest of the bed.

10. Firm down the soil by stepping on the whole area (this turns the pores in the soil from macropores to mesopores, helping it maintain optimum moisture levels).

11. Using a trowel or spade, plant the ferns you have chosen and water them in.

12. Keep them moist throughout the season.

↑
Remove dead or dying fronds when they appear with sharp, clean pruning shears and mulch the plants with a layer of compost during the winter months to provide a rich growing medium for your ferns.

Ferns—various species for a rich assortment, including:
Dicksonia antarctica
Dryopteris spp.
Asplenium spp.
Adiantum spp.
Blechnum (for the harshest climates)
Todea barbara (a favorite of mine but needs protection from frost)

23

OUTDOOR TERRARIUM

🕐 **1 HOUR**

Terrariums are fantastic little curios for the home and garden; they make wonderful, low-maintenance containers and are best suited to either small fern species, if you keep them moist, or succulent species, if you keep them dry.

Most glass containers are suitable for this project but remember that the larger your container, the more plants you need to fill it. Generally, terrariums are round because this is a really effective shape for recycling water—the glass at the top catches the condensation and allows it to drip back onto the plants. However, any shaped terrarium will do the same as long as there is enough room between the plants and the top of the glass. The one thing that is nonnegotiable is that your terrarium must have a hole in it for ventilation. Whether you are growing succulents, ferns, or mosses, this hole is vital to prevent the container from overheating and becoming too moist. In hot, moist conditions, bacteria will thrive, succulents will rot, and ferns will simply overheat.

YOU WILL NEED

Gravel

Funnel

Glass container with a
    ventilation hole

Multipurpose soil (with no topsoil)

Activated charcoal

Stones

Dibber or stick

Plants of your choice
    (fern species, mosses, or
    succulents work nicely)

METHOD

1. Put a layer of gravel in the bottom of the container; use a funnel so that you keep the terrarium's sides clean. Add soil (free from topsoil) above the gravel layer, again using a funnel. Add activating charcoal to the soil to keep the water pure.

2. Dampen the soil and gravel but don't get them too wet—terrariums reuse their water but do not lose an awful lot.

3. Create layers to add interest to your terrarium. To do this, simply mound up the soil toward the back, adding stones to support it, to create a miniature mountainside.

4. Plant your plants with a dibber or stick; you may struggle to get your hand into the terrarium depending on the size of the container you are using.

5. Plant starting from the back and moving forward so that you don't obscure any plants when you place more in front of them.

6. Once your terrarium is planted, the plants retain water, so keep it out of the rain if possible so that you can control the water level. Shady spots, such as at the base of a wall with rain falling from only a certain direction, or under a tree where very little rain will reach the ground, are naturally dry and thus best suited for this kind of terrarium. You will need to water your terrarium once a week (much less often if you planted succulents) and bring it indoors or into a greenhouse during very wet periods.

TIP: A terrarium creates a microclimate inside its glass dome, which makes it possible to grow more tender species in a temperate climate and to retain moisture in weather that would otherwise be dry. If you do grow something tender outside, though, remember that glass is not the best insulator, so you might want to protect it with a blanket or bring it indoors in winter.

My favorites include:

Succulents *Sempervivum, Echiveria, Crassula,* and *Sedum*

Ferns *Dryopteris, Asplenium,* and *Adiantum*

Moss *Selaginella, Lycopodium,* and *Leucobryum*

24

FRUIT TREES IN CONTAINERS

⏱ 1 HOUR

Fruit trees are not only easy to grow, but they make some of the most attractive trees, particularly those in the rose family (*Rosaceae*), such as apples, cherries, pears, almonds, apricots, and peaches. They produce rose-like blossom in the spring, usually ranging from white through soft pinks and into deep cherry red. Many also have brightly colored spring foliage to boot. And, of course, they all produce fruit, although not all are edible, so make sure you know what you are growing.

Lots of fruit trees in the family *Rosaceae* also produce some impressive autumn colors. They are wonderful plants to grow and will flourish in pots. In fact, a pot will restrict the growth of the tree, which means you can even grow a fruit tree on a balcony or small rooftop garden.

An interesting option, although it is not in the rose family, is blueberry. This is an increasingly popular plant to grow because blueberries are very good for you, the plants are hardy and easy to grow, and they need an ericaceous—or acidic—soil. If you don't have this type of soil, you will have to grow them in pots anyway.

YOU WILL NEED

Multipurpose soil (ericaceous for blueberries)
Slow-release fertilizer—a manure, such as pelleted chicken manure or seasoned horse or cow manure, or a granular form of fertilizer
Pottery pieces
A pot—any kind will do, but generally you should get the largest pot you can accommodate/afford because more soil means more valuable nutrients for flowers and fruit
Peach tree—research cultivars that you know to be very tasty. 'Arctic Supreme,' 'Belle of Georgia,' and 'Empress' (a dwarf specimen) are some of the best.
Gravel for dressing the pot

METHOD

1. Mix the soil with the fertilizer according to the package's instructions.
2. Place a layer of pottery pieces into the pot and add a layer of soil mix.
3. Position the peach tree in the pot and backfill with the remaining soil. Firm the soil by pushing down on the soil's surface around the roots of the plant with your hands and then water well.
4. Feed throughout the growing season, especially when fruit is developing, with a potassium-rich liquid fertilizer and add granular or other slow-release fertilizer during the winter.
5. If you get an abundance of fruit you must thin the fruit a little as the year progresses. In most cases, but especially when nutrients are restricted, as they are in a pot, a plant does not have the energy to ripen hundreds of delicious, big, and juicy fruits, so instead it will make many small, less tasty ones; therefore, reducing the number of fruits means that the ones that develop will be bigger, tastier, and juicier.
6. You may need to bring the pot indoors or into a greenhouse or sheltered space during any frosts. Some fruit trees are hardy but check your cultivar for specific information.

Pollinating your fruit tree:
If you have only one plant,
you can ensure pollination
by going from flower to
flower with a paintbrush in
the spring, when the plant
is in bloom. Using the tip of
a clean paintbrush, brush
the pollen on the end of
the stamens and then go
to a different flower on the
same plant and brush that
pollen onto the stigma. The
more flowers you manage to
fertilize, the more fruit you
will get later in the year.

25

TROPICAL STACK FOR A DULL CORNER

🕐 **AN AFTERNOON**

This display is hardy and can make any space feel tropical. It works best on a patio, particularly near your al fresco dining area—I always think that eating in a tropical atmosphere creates the illusion of warm summer evenings. You don't need to live somewhere warm to grow a display that looks tropical, but if you do, and you have an area that is free from frost yet moist enough to support plant life, you could substitute these plant choices with some more tender alternatives, such as *Dahlia*, *Canna*, bananas, and real ginger rather than the hardy ornamental version. However, for our purposes, because not all of us are lucky enough to live in warm climes, I have used species that are tolerant of temperate climates.

You can use nearly any kind of container to create this feature, but because this project also cleverly incorporates height into your garden, one container must be significantly bigger (about twice the size) than the other two to allow a good planting space around the base of the small container. Only your large container will be seen, so choose a nice one. If you want to save some money, you can use any old container for the smaller central pot and hide a strong plastic pot inside the big pot.

YOU WILL NEED

Three big containers:
    two smaller ones about half
    the size of the biggest
Another container to balance
    the smaller one on
Broken pottery pieces
Soil
Water-retaining crystals
Granular feed
Plants (see below)

METHOD

1. It is best to build this container display in its final position because it is a heavy structure and is potentially a little unstable until the roots of the plants have grown to support it.
2. Place an overturned container in the base of the big container.
3. On top of that, place the other smaller container—it doesn't have to be beautiful because it will be hidden by planting.
4. Place a layer of pottery pieces in both upright containers.
5. Mix the soil with the water-retaining crystals and granular feed as directed on the package instructions.
6. Nearly fill the larger container with soil and add a little to the smaller container.
7. Plant your tallest plant in the smaller container and backfill with more soil.
8. Plant the large container so that it is really full, colorful, and lush. Once you are happy, backfill any gaps with the remaining soil. Water well.
9. Feed throughout the growing season with a granular feed.
10. Cut back the herbaceous plants in the autumn.
11. Prune the shrubs for shape and to remove any dead or diseased material as needed.

← I've chosen *Fatsia japonica* for this and smaller plants for the lower level. I've chosen a heavily toothed elder, *Hedychium* (ornamental ginger), *Rudbeckia*, *Geranium*, and *Hebe*.

POTTED BONSAI FOREST

Bonsai, or *penjing*, as it is known in China, is the ancient practice of restricting a tree's growth by keeping it in a pot. Specimens can live for centuries as perfect miniature replicas of their larger brothers. If you are a nurturing, careful person, this is for you. If you are more a type who likes to throw things in pots or in the ground and let nature take care of the rest, it's best to steer clear of the ancient art of bonsai.

If you are growing bonsai trees, I would highly recommend getting containers specifically designed for this purpose. Trees have roots that grow in a very precise way, and a bonsai container is wide and shallow to mimic this shape—think of a wine glass with the tree canopy taking up the goblet and the roots taking up the space of the base. A very deep pot will contain a lot of wasted soil. Bonsai pots also tend to be glazed so that they retain more water.

YOU WILL NEED

Bonsai tree in a pot
Bonsai pruning shears

METHOD

1. Water only when the soil has begun to get dry and make sure ithat it soaks all the way through the soil. Either soak the plant and pot in a bucket or in the sink, or water from above until water runs through the base of the pot, and then repeat a few minutes later.

2. Feeding is also an important part of bonsai maintenance. You should fertilize through the growing season (spring to autumn) and buy products specifically for bonsai trees.

3. Pruning is also essential. Mainly, in bonsai care, you will prune the roots rather than the tips of the trees. However, always remove any dead or diseased branches and any branches that cross or rub together, and you may want to remove an occasional branch that is unsightly.

4. For bonsai, the soil type you use is crucial, so be sure to buy compost specifically for bonsai. There is also an element of pushing a bonsai tree to its limits, so do not repot too frequently—every few years will do— or your tree will begin to get bigger and less and less like a bonsai.

CUT FLOWERS IN AN UPCYCLED CRATE

🕐 AN AFTERNOON

Any flowers can be cut to decorate our homes, but there are certain species that are especially suitable, such as flowers with strong, long stems that stay healthy for longer in our vases. Then there are more subjective qualities, such as colors that you admire or even scents that you prefer. Having a dedicated area in which to grow flowers in succession means you can cut blooms throughout the seasons. You can do this by growing different flowers in the same container that will bloom at different times, but you will have to plan your pots to achieve this. You also need to choose species so they complement each other when they come into flower; there is no point having a sunflower and a soft yellow lily, for example, that bloom at the same time but look awful next to each other. There is a degree of skill in planning a successful container for cut flowers, but one way of getting around the problems of succession and beautifully matched plants is having more than one container—one for each room of your house, perhaps, or one for bright color combinations and one for cool or pastel colors. This way, you can have the best of both worlds.

In terms of flower choice, think texture. Different textures complement each other, so a fern frond, a sprig of eucalyptus, or even a gently frothing *Gypsophila* might be just the thing to make your rose blooms really stand out. Think about all of these different elements to create a successful design, but it's most important to create a grouping of plants that you love!

TIP: You might find it best, unlike in any other planting schemes, to grow these flowers as you would your vegetables: in rows. If you have them planted in big groups or rows, you always know that you're getting the right flower type, even if the buds haven't quite opened yet, and you have the joy of arranging them beautifully, rather than trying to mimic the natural look of what you already had growing.

YOU WILL NEED

Large wooden crate that is
 big enough to accommodate a
 few different flower species and
 deep enough to grow bulbs and
 herbaceous perennials
Plastic liner
Staple gun
Scissors
Soil
Plants
Bulbs
Granular or any slow-release fertilizer

Combine plants to create
a diverse succession of
complementary species.
Choose colors and species that
you really like because they
will end up in your home, not
just in your garden.

Bulbs
Tulipa 'Queen of the Night'
Narcissus 'Silver Chimes'
Allium caeruleum
Annual seeds
Poppy
Nigella
Cornflower
Perennials
Pink roses
Helenium
Dianthus

METHOD

1. It is best to begin this project in autumn, to maximize production for the following year. Plant the crate when it is in its final position and, if possible, choose a location that is mostly protected from the wind. You want the flower stems to be able to grow tall and straight, without any damage, so choose a sheltered position if you can. Also make sure that the flowers get some sun throughout the day so that the stems can grow straight upward rather than leaning out to find light.

2. Line your container with the plastic liner, using the staple gun to attach it to the sides.

3. Cut holes in the liner at the base to allow drainage.

4. Fill your container with soil up to 6 inches (15 cm) from the surface.

5. Lay out rows of bulbs. In between these rows, lay rows of herbaceous plants. Backfill with the remaining soil.

6. Feed in the spring with manure pellets or another slow-release fertilizer, following the instructions on the package.

7. Cut back any late-flowering perennials in mid-spring (reduce the growth by half). If you would like more blooms, remember that they will be smaller than those not cut back, so you may want to cut only half of them back for a good succession of cut flowers.

8. In spring, sow summer annuals for later in the year (except sweet peas, which can often be more successful if sown the autumn before).

9. Remove flower stems from bulbs when the buds are on the verge of opening.

10. Always cut stems on the diagonal and put them in clean water with plant food to reduce risk of bacterial infection and maximize the life of your cut-flower displays.

11. Once the bulbs are done blooming, plant annual bedding in the rows where the bulbs used to be.

12. Keep moist throughout the summer. Deadhead regularly to keep the flowers blooming.

13. When putting cut flowers in water, always remove lower foliage.

28

BULB DISPLAY IN PAINTED POTS

🕐 **1 HOUR**

Bulbs are the container lover's best friends. They grow in nearly any soil type and need minimal care, and, if you choose your species carefully, they will come back year after year. For some of the more beautiful bulbs, such as tulips, there is a little more effort required, and you may need to replace them every two years, or else they will tend to get smaller and smaller until they stop coming back altogether.

Nowadays, we tend to prefer less bright and less bold bulb displays. I still think that the cheeriness and unabashed jolt of color that you get from these bulbs is delightful. But with careful choices, you can create a feature that is tasteful, subtle, and elegant, and one that will keep coming back with minimal effort. Painting your flower pots may seem extremely obvious, but it's actually a very effective twist on the traditional.

↑

My favorite bulbs include: *Allium hollandicum* 'Purple Sensation,' *Fritillaria meleagris, Nectaroscordum, Camassia* (pink or white), *Narcissus* 'Thalia,' and *Chionodoxa luciliae.*

YOU WILL NEED

Traditional terra-cotta pots (any kind, not necessarily old, rustic ones)
Paint and paintbrush—any long-wearing paint will do (If you want bright colors, acrylic might provide the greatest variety, but if you want classic, more subdued colors, an exterior masonry paint is the most durable.)
Broken pottery pieces
Multipurpose soil
Bulbs

METHOD

1. It is best to begin this project in autumn, when you can buy bulbs, rather than in spring, when the bulbs are already in bloom and are much more expensive as well as less likely to come back looking lovely and healthy the following year. Snowdrops are the only exception because they need to be bought already in bloom and in soil.

2. Paint the bottom or top half to two-thirds of your pots, depending on your taste and the color. If you have chosen a very bright paint color and you want to paint the entire pot, consider planting bulbs that will produce flowers in stronger colors. For half-painted pots, anything with an element of subtlety, such as pale pink, lilac, white, pale or robin's egg blue, gray, or even navy blue (especially with the terra-cotta color) will work nicely. You could always try painting half of the pot initially and then go on to paint the whole thing if you feel that the color combination isn't working.

3. Place a couple of pottery pieces, or even just a few stones, in the bottom of the pot—most bulbs hate to sit in water because it can cause them to rot, especially in winter, so it's best to add extra drainage. You may even want to include some gravel if you are worried about drainage or live in an area with high rainfall.

4. Add soil to the pot until it's about 6 inches (15 cm) from the top.

5. Place the biggest bulbs on this layer— so that's *Allium* and *Camassia*. It is a good rule of thumb that any bulb should be planted at a depth of three times its height. There are a few exceptions, such as hyacinths, which need to be planted on the surface to encourage flowers, but, generally speaking, you can't go too wrong by following this rule. If in doubt, most packages will have planting depths listed.

6. Pour a layer of soil over the tops of the bulbs until the soil is at a depth of about 4 inches (10 cm).

7. Arrange a layer of *Narcissus* and *Nectaroscordum*. Add yet more soil until there is about 2 inches (5 cm) of the pot rim showing.

8. There is no need to water the pots if you leave them outside because the weather should do this for you over the winter months.

9. Feed the bulbs as they are growing with a granular organic fertilizer, which you should water in. Remove any seedheads before they have a chance to fully form. Remove the dead stems once they have turned completely brown and replenish the soil with some fresh soil every year.

10. You may want to add some extra bulbs every autumn to keep your displays looking their best year after year. You should either replace any tulips that have finished flowering or add extras because the tulips will become weaker as the years go on.

29

PICTURE-FRAME SEEDLINGS

🕐 **AN AFTERNOON**

We gardeners take great pride in our plants, and although we secretly like to think of our gardens and our plants as works of art, it is not usually the norm to put them in picture frames. But this method of growing seedlings is a great way of seeing them in their full glory. By growing your seeds this way, you get to see them at every stage of growth, from germination to right up to the point when they are ready to be transplanted. Anything with shallow roots, such as alpines, succulents, Mediterranean herbs, and mosses, would be happy in this type of container as long as it is kept well watered. This is also a fun way of engaging kids in the process of growing while also educating them about nature and science. It's infinitely fascinating for us adults, too!

YOU WILL NEED

Piece of thin plywood
Picture frame at least 1.25 inches (about 3 cm deep, with picture and glass removed)
Waterproof paint (any color you like, but darker colors work particularly well)
Paintbrush
Plexiglass (cut to two-thirds the height of the picture frame)
Drill
Wood screws
Hooks for back of picture frame
Strong exterior wire
Picture hook
Hammer
Nail
Seed-starting soil (or multipurpose if you are growing something else)
Seeds of your choice

METHOD

1. Cut a piece of plywood the same size as the back of the picture frame.
2. Paint the plywood and the inside of the frame with your chosen color and let it dry for two hours or until the paint is bone dry. Any dampness means that soil will stick to the paint.
3. Insert the plexiglass into the place where the glass would normally go, leaving the gap at the top.
4. Screw the plywood to the back of the frame using a drill and wood screws.
5. Drill three to four drainage holes into the underside of the frame.
6. Attach the hooks and wire to the back of the picture frame. Hooks and eyes for picture frames usually screw in on their own, so you can do this by hand rather than with a drill. Thread the wire through and double it back on itself, twisting it around itself.
7. Put a picture hook in the wall with a hammer and nail.
8. Hang up the frame, putting the middle point of the wire on the hook and making sure it is level.
9. Fill the frame with soil, leaving a gap of about an inch/a few centimeters at the top.
10. Sprinkle or sow your seeds following the instructions on the seed packets. Water well and make sure they stay moist. Watch them grow!
11. Prick out the seedlings once the second set of leaves has grown. If you have left a third of the top space free, you should be able to do this with a dibber or a pencil. Otherwise, carefully remove the frame from the wall and unscrew the plywood so that you can access the seedlings.

For extra-healthy edibles, grow microgreens in your picture frame and harvest them at this stage. Coriander, pea shoots, radishes, cabbage, leeks, and mustard will work well.

PROJECTS

131

30

OLD CABINET WITH BURNT ORANGE AND BLUES

🕐 **AN AFTERNOON**

What could be more magical, or unusual, than furniture turned into containers? We all have old pieces in our homes or sheds that we no longer use, so it's time to resurrect them and turn them into something new. This project works best with a chest of drawers, but any cabinet can be turned into something useful and beautiful.

Wooden furniture will probably need a regular coat of varnish or wood preservative, before you plant it, if you want it to have a long life in your garden. I love blue and orange because they evoke a sense of rustiness and look eclectically modern—natural but strangely unnatural. These are contrasting colors, and few plants are naturally bright blue, making them feel unearthly, yet the rusty color of burnt orange creates a scheme very much in nature. For an old cabinet, this is a great color combination that makes a striking design feature.

YOU WILL NEED

Old chest of drawers, dresser, or cabinet of any size that fits the space you have to fill. It can be made of wood (which needs treating to protect it from the elements), metal, or plastic. One with three drawers works best to allow the plants plenty of room to grow.
Wood preservative and paintbrush
Drill
Plastic liner
Screws and screwdriver
Multipurpose soil
Plants

I'm using blues and oranges:
Eryngium
Agapanthus
Lobelia erinus 'Blue Cascade'
Festuca glauca 'Elijah Blue'
Carex 'Red Rooster'
Crocosmia (common montbretia)
Ceratostigma
Anemanthele lessoniana
Hardy blue *Geranium*
Lavandula angustifolia
Libertia peregrinans

METHOD

1. Remove the drawers. If you are using a wooden chest, treat the entire thing with varnish or wood preservative.

2. Drill drainage holes into each drawer at intervals of about 2.75 inches (7 cm).

3. Line each drawer that you intend to plant with plastic and make holes in the liner that correspond with the holes in the drawer. If you have a classic three-drawer chest, the best way to plant it is by planting the top and bottom drawers but leave the middle drawer unplanted for reasons of weight distribution.

4. Replace the drawers with the lowest one sticking out the farthest and the top one open equivalent to the width of one plant.

5. Screw the drawers into position so there is no chance of their falling out once weighed down with plants.

6. Fill each drawer with soil.

7. Arrange your plants in the drawers, placing the cascading plants, such as hardy *Geranium*, so that they disguise the edges. Water well.

8. Keep your plants moist throughout the season by watering them during dry, hot periods. There is little need to deadhead these species, with the exception of Lobelia; if you keep the flower seeds on for as long as possible into the winter, it will provide food for the birds.

For extra security, weigh or screw down your cabinet to prevent it from falling over.

31

WINTER POT

🕐 **AN AFTERNOON**

It is a strange phenomenon that the most fragrant plants grow best in shade. This is because insects struggle to see flowers in the dark shadows of trees, so if plants can lure insects with their sweet smells, there is more chance of their being pollinated. Often, shade lovers will also have white flowers to make them as visible as possible, and the combination of white flowers and a heady scent can make a great feature. What better way to make use of a shady corner of the yard or garden? There are also a host of plants that flower in the winter or late autumn and give delicate splashes of color in the depths of the season.

Here I've planted one such flowering plant, *Chrysanthemum*, in a cement pot that I created using a wok as my mold and a dryish cement mix. The beauty of this is that in shady conditions, it will grow a rich layer of moss on it, creating a beautifully natural and aged look.

YOU WILL NEED

Stone trough—something that will age nicely and get a lovely covering of moss over time. If you don't have a stone container, you can make your own using concrete, petroleum jelly, and a wok (see Method).

Multipurpose soil

Plants

METHOD

1. Mix some mortar to make a dryish, still grainy (definitely not wet) mix.
2. Cover an old wok in petroleum jelly.
3. Line the wok with mortar mix around 1.5 inches (3–4 cm) thick. Leave a hole in the center for drainage; this will be doable if your cement mix is dry enough.
4. After forty-eight hours of dry conditions, remove the concrete from the wok. It should fall out easily if there was enough petroleum jelly in the wok.

HOW TO PLANT

1. If you are planting a single specimen, like *Chrysanthemum,* then place it in isolation in the pot. The round form of *Chrysanthemum* will echo the rounded shape of the wok. It makes a fantastic impact.
2. Keep the soil moist but not wet and feed with a granular fertilizer every few months.
3. Place the stone trough in a corner of the yard or garden that gets shade or partial sun. If the wall or fence above it gets more sun, then a clematis will flower prolifically. (If there is no sun, replace the clematis with ivy— the flowers may not be as strongly scented, but they provide some perfume at the end of the summer, and bees go crazy for them.)
4. Fill the trough with soil nearly to the top.
5. Plant the clematis at the back and attach it to the wall behind. In front of the clematis, plant the *Daphne odora*. Fill the entire front of the trough with lily-of-the-valley and then water in. If you made the container using a wok, leave out the clematis because it needs deep root space, which this homemade stone trough won't provide.
6. Because the plants in this container are fairly long lived, you need to replace the soil every few years and transplant the plants about every five years to allow each species plenty of growing room. If you don't have the room to do this, growing just a *Daphne odora* or a lily-of-the-valley will provide shady scent without the need for regular transplanting.

For winter scent
Daphne odora
Convallaria majalis
  (lily-of-the-valley)
Clematis armandii
For winter flowers
Chrysathemum
Galanthus nivalis
Winter aconite
Primula
Cyclamen hederifolium

135

32

RUSTIC STONE POT FILLED WITH ACID-LOVING PLANTS

🕐 **1 HOUR**

There are different kinds of soil, and each type makes a perfect home for different kinds of plants. Acidic soil is one of the most common, and most plants prefer soil to be ever-so-slightly acidic rather than ever-so-slightly alkaline. When we talk about acid lovers, though, we mean plants that really need acidic conditions—or at least plants that are pretty uncomfortable in an alkaline soil. To get an idea of these species, you need to imagine a mountain or a moor. In these conditions, where the soil is in close proximity to the rock below (unless that rock is a form of limestone), the soil will tend to be very acidic. Anything that grows there will grow in your acidic pot. We typically think of *rhododendrons, camellias,* and other such species for these conditions, but there are other, more interesting, species, that prefer acidic positions, too. To recreate this environment in the garden, I devised a project that is rustic and naturalistic to create a little piece of heaven for acid-loving plants.

Using Stones
Porous stones hold on to more moisture, but use whatever stones you have in your area because this makes buying them cheaper, and they look more at home in your garden. Alternatively, if you have concrete areas or pavers, match the stones to this. The only stones that are not appropriate are limestones; these are alkaline and will affect the health of the acid-loving plants.

YOU WILL NEED
Stones—preferably large and flat, but any kind will do. The amount of stones you need depends on the size of the stones and the size of your space.
Ericaceous (acidic) soil
Acid-loving plants: *Acer, Pieris, Erica, Dryopteris* (or any others you like, including *Magnolia, Cedrus, Ceanothus, Molinia, Loropetalum, Cornus, Viburnum, Sorbus, Skimmia,* and many more)

METHOD
1. Arrange your stones in a circular shape and build up to a height that you feel is stable and secure to make a container. (You can shore it up with mortar, if you like, but this will decrease its acidity.) You will need to protect *Acer* and ferns from full sunshine and strong winds, so place the stone circle in a suitable position.
2. Fill the stone container, including any gaps in the stones, with ericaceous soil, almost to the top.
3. Plant your chosen species in the container, including in the gaps in the stones, and then water well.
4. Add a mulch of ericaceous soil every year to keep the species looking healthy. Prune as needed to keep the plants' shapes attractive. Remove any dead, dying, or diseased branches.

To change things up, you could try one of these different planting combinations: *Acer*, *Pieris*, and *Loropetalum chinense*. *Ceanothus* and *Dryopteris* (keep it simple with blues and greens). *Cornus* with *Molinia* (something with red coloration like 'Edith Dudszus' looks breathtaking against the red stems of *Cornus alba*). *Sorbus aucuparia* ('Copper Kettle' is beautiful, S. *vilmorinii* is a personal favorite, and the classic red berries of mountain ash look great) with *Molinia* and *Erica* in drifts looks fantastic in a large container. *Cedrus glauca* gets huge in the ground, but its growth is restricted in a pot, and it looks wonderful underplanted with shade-tolerant ferns such as *Dryopteris* and white-flowered *Calluna*.

33

TURN A GARBAGE CAN INTO SOMETHING MORE PRODUCTIVE

🕐 **1 HOUR**

Outdoor garbage cans are just as much a part of our households as our family pets. They often jostle with our cars (and the cars of people who come to visit) for the limited space in front of our homes. We often try to come up with ingenious ways of hiding these eyesores and spend considerable amounts of money doing so. We build sheds around them, decorate them, and erect fences in front of them. But the way I see it, these trash cans are essentially huge containers, so rather than going to great lengths to hide them, flaunt them (not the ones you need for your garbage and recycling, but any old or extra ones). If one of your trash cans gets a little broken or develops a hole, so much the better. There are a number of vegetables that positively thrive in such conditions, particularly ones that grow long in either direction—root vegetables, including parsnips and carrots, as well as the leafy vegetable I'm focusing on: leeks.

YOU WILL NEED

Old garbage can (preferably with wheels), at least 3 feet (about 1 m) tall
Drill
Multipurpose soil
Dibber
Leeks (pencil thickness, ready to plant—either seedlings you've grown yourself or ones you've bought) Sow leeks in spring and transplant them into their final positions in early summer.
Granular slow-release fertilizer

METHOD

1. Drill some drainage holes into the bottom of your old trash can; four decent-sized holes should be enough to let excess water escape.
2. Fill the can with soil about three-fifths full (just over halfway) and firm the soil.
3. With a dibber, make holes in the soil about 6 inches (15 cm) apart and drop one leek into each.
4. Water and feed the leeks regularly throughout the growing season with a high-nitrogen fertilizer such as chicken-manure pellets.
5. Harvest the leeks from the end of the summer right through the winter, when they will be big enough to eat, but before they have gone to flower.

34

UPCYCLED CHAIR WITH DEEP PURPLES AND SILVERS

🕐 **AN AFTERNOON**

There is a lot of aesthetic value in old furniture, and even modern pieces have something to offer if you have the vision to turn them into something more interesting. What better way to revitalize them than to mix antique pieces with something natural? Chairs make great upcycled containers because, as well as adding greenery, you are adding a bit of sculpture and height to your garden. Creating varying levels keeps the eye interested, and that can really bring a small space to life.

A purple and silver planting combination is ever-so-slightly magical. Plants in these colors tend to have a certain delicate air that others lack. Plants with silver foliage go well with any other color and provide interest even when they are not in bloom. In a small space like a container, where plant choices are limited, this adds a great deal of aesthetic value. Pale colors, such as silver, also reflect light and bounce well off other colors without stealing the show. Purple marries effortlessly and naturally with silver and echoes this dainty style, with *Allium* and little *Campanula* flowerheads creating the same fairy-like feel. You could also use any bright color.

Bulbs

Allium hollandicum 'Purple
  Sensation'
Tulipa 'Queen of Night'
Iris reticulata 'Katharine
  Hodgkin'
Heuchera 'Palace Purple'
Sedum sieboldii

Perennial plants

Artemisia schmidtiana
Verbena bonariensis
Nepeta x *faassenii*

YOU WILL NEED

Old chair—wood or metal works best
  because it can withstand the weather.
  You can use an old upholstered chair,
  but it will become damp and probably
  moldy, maybe even sprouting some
  fungi after a season or two, and
  eventually rotting. I would stick to
  wood or metal.
Strong burlap
Drill
Soil
Water-retaining crystals
Bulbs and perennial plants (see left)
Staple gun

METHOD

1. Start this project in the autumn,
    when bulbs are at their cheapest
    and they have a few months to settle
    in. Remove the seat of the chair by
    cutting it off and lifting it out. Some
    wooden seats can simply be pried off.
    Avoid damaging the chair itself.
2. Make a strong, deep bowl of burlap
    (strong enough to house plants, soil,
    and water) where the seat was. You
    may need to double or even triple the
    layers of burlap in order to guarantee
    its strength. Staple it to the seat.
3. Mix the soil with the water-retaining
    crystals according to the package's
    instructions.
4. Put a thin layer of soil in the bottom of
    your container.
5. Place the *alliums* and tulips on the
    layer of soil. Sprinkle more soil on top
    so that the bulbs are almost covered.
6. Around the bulbs, place your
    perennial plants. Be sure to allow the
    bulbs beneath space to grow up, so try
    to avoid putting perennials directly on
    top of them.
7. Fill the spaces around the root balls
    with the remaining soil.
8. Push the *Iris reticulata* very gently Into
    the gaps between the plants.
9. Water the plants well. Keep the soil
    moist but not wet; these plants like
    fairly dry conditions. (Remember that,
    for container planting, it is important
    to choose plants that complement
    each other in terms of their preferred
    conditions.)
10. In the spring and summer, as soon as
    the bulbs have gone brown, cut
    off the foliage to make the best
    summer display.

35

MOSS TEACUPS

🕐 **1 HOUR**

Moss is in high demand. Garden designers who have been using cushion moss (white moss) in Japanese-inspired reflection gardens and alongside cobblestone have inspired the horticultural world. However, it is important to acquire moss from sustainable sources; in some places, is illegal to take moss from the woods, as a means of protecting native species in the wild. You can buy sustainably grown moss from all sorts of places; it is even being introduced in prison systems as a way of encouraging free enterprise for prisoners. There is ongoing research into growing moss sustainably, so please support these endeavors.

Teacups make great features on their own; I love teacups and have an unfortunate habit of collecting them. I also make pottery, especially teacups, so I find that my collection is growing to unsustainable numbers! As a way of using them more effectively, I started to grow plants in them. Moss is a great choice for this because the cups offer such limited space, and I love the lush, verdant, and varying choice it provides.

YOU WILL NEED

Old china teacup and saucer
Moisture-retentive soil or compost
Sustainably sourced moss—the most
  attractive mosses for a container include
  cushion (white) moss (*Leucobryum*),
  upright moss (*Polytrichum*),
  sphagnum moss (*Sphagnum*), club
  moss (*Lycopodium*) and spike moss
  (*Selaginella*), though there are many
  more interesting species if you can find
  a specialty grower.

METHOD

1. Fill the cup with the soil or compost. Generally, moss likes the shade, where it is damp. You might find that compost-filled cups placed in shady areas of the garden naturally begin to form moss of their own, but if you bought moss and are in doubt about where to put your containers, damp shade is usually best.
2. Place the moss carefully on top of the soil or compost.
3. Give a good watering.
4. It will need to be kept permanently moist but not wet, so keep an eye on it.

PROJECTS

143

36

UPCYCLED CONTAINER CHAIRS

🕐 **AN AFTERNOON**

Outdoor furniture, like it or not, has become part of our daily lives. Housing costs are on the rise, and we often find ourselves struggling with limited space. Outdoor areas are therefore increasingly valued, and we have begun to use them as extensions of our homes. We eat outside, we sit outside, and some people even sleep outside from time to time. A yard gives us extra room, but all too often our outdoor furniture can be something of an eyesore. There are some lovely pieces of outdoor furniture available if you are willing to spend a lot, and the cheaper they, are the less stylish they tend to be, however useful. So here's a good solution: why not try making your own homegrown outdoor furniture? There are all sorts of plants you can sit or lie on. Some, like chamomile, are beautifully scented and can be used in all kinds of ways, including cosmetics and tea, and can be grown on all types of surfaces to make ingenious seating. So, with practicality and beauty to gain, there isn't much to lose. I'm using thyme, which is incidentally one of my favorite culinary herbs, too!

YOU WILL NEED

Piece of old plywood
Pen/pencil
Saw
Old car tire—you can get them inexpensively from garages or junkyards
Wood screws
Drill
Pea gravel
Soil
Chamomile, or another plant that can be trampled, such as thyme or even turf

METHOD

1. Cut the plywood into a circle to fit the tire. Measure it by placing the tire on top of the wood and drawing around it (a hexagon works as well as a circle and is easier to cut). For an extra-long life, you might want to varnish your plywood.
2. Screw the plywood onto the tire withwood screws that go through the plywood and straight into the tire.
3. Drill some drainage holes into the plywood about every 3 inches (7 cm or so). Most trample-proof plants require free-draining soil, so you can't overdo the holes as long as you don't compromise the strength of the plywood.
4. Combine the soil with the gravel in a 50:50 mix.
5. Fill the tire almost to the top with soil and then firm it down well.
6. Make small holes in the soil and put the plants into the holes so that there is good coverage but still about an inch/a few centimeters around each plant for the roots to grow. Water in.
7. Keep watered but not too much—if the seat is outside, the rain should do the job.

FIVE WAYS TO TRANSFORM A PLASTIC POT

We all have plastic pots lying around and, annoyingly, every time we buy another plant, we get another pot. But with a little ingenuity and creativity, you can turn them into something much more beautiful. It doesn't take a lot of time or skill—just a few simple tricks will make your plastic pots into something to be proud of.

Generally, giving these pots a facelift requires some messy materials, so you may want to lay down newspaper or plastic sheets before you begin. The most basic method of transformation is painting; it's simple and effective, and by layering and distressing the paint, you can create an expensive-looking container. For a more personalized look, you can adorn your painted pots with words, such as your name or a quote or phrase that means a lot to you. More skillful painters can do this by hand, but stencils will work just as well.

The next step up from painting is sticking things to your pots. It may sound a bit preschool-ish, but it can actually look very attractive. With a paper napkin, some old string, or some sand, the transformation becomes easy and effective.

DÉCOUPAGE WITH NAPKINS ⏱ A WEEKEND

WHAT YOU WILL NEED

Paper napkins—plain or patterned,
    depending on your taste
Plastic pots
Waterproof PVA/all-purpose glue
    (suitable for exteriors)
Paintbrush

METHOD

1. Tear or cut the paper napkins into
   thin strips. The smaller the strips, the
   neater the finished project will be, but
   using big pieces creates more texture
   and gets the job done more quickly.
2. Cover the pot in glue with a
   paintbrush. Stick a layer of napkin
   strips all over the pot. Cover the
   layer of napkins with glue, using a
   paintbrush. Stick on another layer of
   torn-up napkins amd then coat with
   another layer of glue.
3. Let it dry. Drying should take twelve
   to twenty-four hours, depending on
   the conditions.
4. Plant the pot with any plants you like.
   For heavily decorative découpage,
   foliage-driven plants like alpines (I've
   used *Raoulia*) or even mosses work
   nicely, but for simpler designs, you
   can let the plants and flowers speak
   for themselves by using shrubs with
   interesting foliage colors and plants
   with flowers. Scents are great, either
   foliage or flower, no matter what color
   and pattern your paper is.

Clockwise from top
left: moss, *Raoulia*,
and *Cotinus* in
découpage pots.

PAINTED AND AGED 🕐 AN AFTERNOON

YOU WILL NEED

Plastic pots
Paintbrush
Paint—waterproof or exterior
masonry paint works best.
Two related but slightly
different tones will create
an aged look.
Old fork or steel wool
Sponge

METHOD

1. Paint on a thick layer of color—grays and whites work nicely because closely related colors blend well. Gray creates a stone-like effect, while bright colors are more unnatural but more fun and unusual.

2. Using an old fork or some steel wool, remove and cross-hatch parts of the paint while it's still wet.

3. Once the paint has dried (it should take a couple of hours but check the paint can for drying times), speckle on extra color with the sponge. A slightly different tone works well to create a naturally aged finish. Once this layer is dry, you may want to go over patches with the original color to even out the tone.

4. Plant your pot with any plant of your choice. When it comes to plastic pots, the simpler the plant, the better, especially if you've decorated your pot. Whether you created a natural stone finish or a brighter, more exotic look, something like a fern or other foliage plant, such as *Pachysandra terminalis* or *Vinca minor,* with its sporadic blue flowers, will enhance the pot without making the whole arrangement too busy.

STENCILED LETTERS ⏱ AN AFTERNOON

YOU WILL NEED

Plastic pots
Multipurpose spray paint
(available from most
hardware, home-
improvement, and craft-
supply stores in all kinds
of colors)
Stencils
Sponge (optional)
Waterproof paint (optional)

METHOD

1. Spray the pot with multipurpose spray paint. For a tasteful look, choose subtle colors such as white on a pale blue background or gray on white. If you are making personalized pots, particularly for children, allow them to choose their own colors to make the pots even more personal.

2. Decide on the word or phrase you want to feature; it could be the name of the plant(s) you are growing (for example, a collection of herbs) or the name of the person who will be using the pot. It could be your house number if you intend to put the pot by the front door.

3. Stencil the chosen word to the front of the pot using spray paint in a contrasting color or a sponge dipped in waterproof paint.

4. Wait two to four hours for the containers to dry. (Always check the paint cans for specific drying times.)

5. Plant the pots with the plants of your choice. Because the pots are decorative, keeping the planting simple creates an effective design. Your color schemes will also dictate what you plant; green goes with any bright color, so a foliage-heavy design will enhance the pot, while contrasting colors create a striking look. A purple pot is springs to life with yellow flowers, orange goes with blue, and so on.

SANDBLASTED 🕐 A WEEKEND

YOU WILL NEED

Plastic pots
Waterproof/all-purpose PVA glue
    (suitable for exteriors)
Paintbrush
Sand (plain or colored)
Ribbon or string (optional)

METHOD

1. Cover your plastic pot in glue with a paintbrush.
2. Roll the glue-covered pot in your chosen sand.
3. Wait up to twenty-four hours for it to dry and set.
4. Plant the pot. The color of sand you use (see below) might dictate what you plant. If you chose a plain, light-colored sand, you will have a blank canvas that works with most plants, whether foliage or flowers. If you chose a red sand, something rustic and traditional, similar to what you'd find in a terra-cotta pot, might work best. Using colored sand makes the pot more of a design feature, so you might want to keep your planting simple.
5. For a pretty finish, tie a ribbon or string around the pot.

Choosing your sand Sand comes in many colors and textures. Builder's sharp sand may be grayish, yellowish, or reddish in color, with bigger bits of grit. Kiln-dried sand is much paler and finer, which gives a smoother effect. You can use red sand for a terra-cotta feel.

ROPED UP 🕐 A WEEKEND

YOU WILL NEED

Plastic pots
Super glue (such as Krazy Glue®)
Hot glue gun and glue sticks
Rope, string, or wool
Paintbrush
Waterproof PVA /all-purpose glue
(suitable for exteriors)

METHOD

1. The thinner the rope or string, the more times you will need to wrap it around the pot, so you'll need a longer length. Thicker rope or string needs a more generous dose of glue and maybe some hidden nails to hold in place. Wool can work nicely, but make sure you coat it with all-purpose glue after you stick it to the pot.

2. Apply super glue around the bottom edge of the outside of the pot.

3. Attach the string to the glued area so that it encircles the pot. Keep wrapping the string around the pot and, as you move up the pot, add hot glue to each layer you are about to wrap. Continue all the way to the top and over the rim so that the pot is completely covered.

4. Use a paintbrush to apply all-purpose glue over the whole thing and allow it to dry for up to twenty-four hours.

5. Plant the pot with something simple. In a small pot, a herbaceous perennial with interesting foliage, like *Sedum, Phormium*, palms, *Pachysandra, Galium odoratum*, or *Filipendula* will do very nicely. Deep colors like reds or purples mixed with little bits of silver can work very well. *Eryngium, Dianthus*, nasturtium, *Dahlia, Papaver, Lavandula, Fuchsia, Aster*, and *Salvia* would all look beautiful.

The decorative nature of this pot lends itself to simple, foliage-heavy planting. Depending on the size of your pot, you may want to use a fern or tree fern; a small shrub, like *Ruscus*, *Hebe*, *Nandina*, or *Skimmia*; or a fruit tree, like blueberry.

MAINTENANCE

By now, it should be clear to you that, as a container gardener, the onus is on you to keep your pots and plants looking good, but don't forget that a container is manageable—it is compact and controllable. Essentially, it's *contained*!

Every plant must work hard and earn its place in your container, though, and that's also where you come in; plants cannot be expected simply to sit there, doing their best, looking their prettiest, without a helping hand from you—a gentle nudge in the right direction. Your work is much easier for containers kept outside because the rain will water them for you and the sun will shine on them but not bake them.

The biggest maintenance issue for you is that the plants' true nature is being restricted. In a container, a plant may have only a small area of soil to feed from, year after year after year, yet you expect it to perform for you—to flower, to fruit, to produce more and more foliage, and give off delicious scents. It is up to you to make sure that the conditions in that small space give the plant everything it needs to thrive.

REFRESHING THE SOIL

There are two key components to keeping a plant happy: nutrients and moisture (without which, the nutrients cannot be assimilated into a plant's roots). Soil holds both of these elements and, as you might expect, the quantities needed of each vary according to the particular plant.

The problem with soil in containers is that, in a limited space, the goodness from the soil is used up fairly quickly, depending on the size of the container, Even if you are supplementing the soil with fertilizers, it is still a good idea to refresh the soil every year or two.

It's not a tricky job; all you have to do is take the plant or plants out of the container, shake off the soil from the roots and set them aside, and make sure that the plants' roots don't dry out while they're out of the pot. You then need to remove the soil left in the pot (a little more challenging with a large pot!) and replace it with fresh soil. Once the pot is full again, replace the plants and immediately water the newly filled pots so that the roots can make contact with the new soil.

It's a good idea to refresh the soil of outdoor containers in the winter, when the plants are dormant and therefore won't be disturbed by the upheaval. If it is very cold, do this in a shed or garage (preferably somewhere unheated) rather than outside so that the roots don't freeze.

REPOTTING

Repotting is basically moving a plant from one pot to another, often larger, one. It is about replenishing the growing medium as well as increasing the plant's available space tby putting it into a bigger container.

The best times to repot depend on what you're growing and the stage of the plants' growth. If a plant has been happy for a long time in its container but begins to do poorly, consider repotting it. However, before you do so, try reinvigorating it with new soil and see if that does the trick. If a plant that should naturally be a large species looks very sad, or if it starts to topple over in the wind because it has become a bit top-heavy, go straight to repotting.

A seedling needs to be repotted regularly. It should be "pricked out" (gently removed from its pot using a dibber while holding one of the leaves) as soon as its true leaves (second set of leaves) form and then put into successively bigger pots as soon as the roots begin to show through the holes at the base of the container. An annual plant, for example, tends to be bigger and better the larger the container that it's in. In a hanging basket, you'll pot the seedling from a plug straight into its final position and let it grow to fill its space, but for most other containers, you'll put a plant you have grown from seed into successively bigger pots until it's in its final pot.

For slower-growing plants or plants that you have grown from seed but are now mature specimens, you'll need to repot far less often. As a container gardener, choosing the size of container gives you control over the growth of your plants. It is certainly not a matter of life and death if you do not repot your plants. In fact, it's quite the opposite—you need to decide whether you want your plants to express their true nature (as they will in as big a container as you can find) or you use the container to restrict and control their growth to make them better suit your needs. Also consider that some species (*Agapanthus* being the most notable) actually thrive in a restricted environment. The more root-bound, the better the flowers will be on your *Agapanthus* plants. Not only that, but they do not like their roots to be disturbed, so if you repot them, they will take some time to recover and may even not flower. (There are only a few examples of such plants. *Agapanthus* is the most noteworthy and well known example because these kinds of plants are few and far between, though nearly all alpines thrive with restricted roots.)

FEEDING

How much or how little you should feed your plants varies a lot from species to species. If you are growing plants to harvest and eat, they will generally require more feeding than other plants. See page 56 for specifics, but generally a fruiting or flowering plant will need a high dose of potassium, a leafy plant will require nitrogen, and a root plant will require phosphorus.

The one thing to remember is that, in a container, a plant gets all of its food from you. In nature, there are all kinds of mechanisms for providing plants with nutrients, which are lacking in the less-than-natural environment of a plant pot. In a raised bed, there will be more nutrient availability, and if that raised bed sits on earth in your yard rather than on concrete or similar, it will benefit even more from nutrients. Generally, though, as a container gardener it is up to you to make sure that your potted plants are fed properly. Replacing the soil annually may do the job for you. You might also add a little manure to seep down through the soil and keep your plants in good health. This might be all that your containers require, but many of us grow floral, hardworking plants, which can be a little hungrier.

I recommend that you refresh your containers' soil on an annual or biennial basis and then, for cropping or flowering plants, add a slow-release fertilizer in the spring and then a liquid feed every couple of weeks throughout the growing season. Your containers may need more or less rigorous feeding, but research the requirements for the species you grow and remember that the rule of thumb is usually the smaller the container, the more you will need to do to keep the plants healthy.

CLEAN AS YOU GO

It sounds boring, but containers can be a bit of an annoyance if they become too dirty. They can trap leaves, dust, and debris behind them and, after sitting in the same place awhile, getting watered periodically, with soil falling down their sides, their exteriors can get a bit grubby, too. So get in there and give them a cleaning every few months—you can simply hose down the containers' exteriors and the ground around them when you're watering, or you can move the containers, wipe them down, and sweep the areas. You will find that regular cleaning will make your garden or yard look brighter, fresher, and generally better.

WATERING

Water is essential for plant growth. All plants need some moisture, but how much depends on the species. In a temperate climate, plants require water every few days, but remember that it is easier to kill a plant by watering it too much than by not watering it enough. The bigger the container, the less you have to water it, and you definitely do not want your plants to be sitting in water because if soil is permanently moist, it becomes devoid of oxygen and toxic to plants. Bog plants and water plants are exception because they have evolved adaptations that enable them to deal with these conditions.

Generally, you are aiming for a moist but free-draining environment that gives the plants just enough moisture. If you make a plant work hard for its moisture, it will be tougher in the long run and will rely less on water than one that gets a good drink every day.

AUTOMATIC WATERING SYSTEMS

We've all been away on vacation or for work and suddenly realized that our beloved plants have been left without any water and may all be wilting, if not dead, upon our return. It's heartbreaking to get home and see all of your precious progeny lying flat on their shriveled faces on their parched, baked soil. But worry not—there are some little tricks I've learned to prevent this devastation.

- **Shoelaces:** A bottle filled with water with a shoelace dipped in it (right to the bottom) and then pushed into the soil of each pot releases a slow-drip feed to your plants.

- **An irrigation system:** For those with some money to spend, an irrigation system guarantees that there is always moisture in the soil. Such a system may be solar powered, or it can be connected to a rain barrel, or it can measure the moisture content of the soil so that it only waters when needed. Very clever!

- **An overturned bottle:** Fill a bottle with water and stick it upside-down in the soil. You can either remove the lid completely or make a little hole in the lid to release the water into the soil, depending how quickly or slowly you want the water to be released.

- **Drip trays:** Make sure that you leave a little water, about 1 inch (2.5 cm), in the drip tray. That will give you an extra couple of days during which you won't have to water.

- **Leave your pots in the bathtub:** When I'm away for a while, I bring my most prized pots inside, leave about 2 inches (5 cm) of water in the bathtub, and put the pots in there. It isn't a great idea for a long time, but, for a week or so, it's a lifeline.

- **Leave them outside:** There's at least a 50 percent chance of rain, right?

DEADHEADING AND CUTTING BACK

As with all plants, maintaining your container specimens to a high standard helps them perform better. Potted plants have to earn their space even more than plants in the rest of the garden because a container is a natural showcase. There are some basic points to remember to help you with plant maintenance.

The first is deadheading: cutting the dead flowers off the plants. This may not be necessary with all species—some flower repeatedly, others don't; some produce fruit and seeds, others don't. So get to know your species. Certain plants will produce flowers prolifically according to how much you deadhead (think sweet peas, cosmos, dahlias, and most other types of bedding plants), while some need the dead flowers left on in order to perform some other function, be it fruit or seed

or hips. There is no point in spending hours deadheading when there is no need, but for plants that do respond well to this treatment, it is an essential maintenance task. A little time spent snipping off the old flowers means that your containers won't be full of brown, messy, old flower heads, and will also increase the flowering window of your plants, helping them to earn their place in your garden.

Another important job for container growers is pruning. Again, how much or how little varies considerably according to what you've planted. A bonsai, for example, will need to be pruned by the roots and only on the top to remove dead branches; a box hedge will need pruning once or twice a year to remove the tips and reshape; and a herbaceous perennial will need to be cut back right to the ground during the winter. But there are a few hard-and-fast rules that can guide you (see right).

HOW TO PRUNE

- Cut away any part of the plant that is dead, dying, or diseased.

- Remove crossing branches on any shrub to encourage an open habit (this allows air to circulate around the plant and prevents diseases from taking hold).

- Generally, though not in every single case (*Clematis, Wisteria,* and silver birch being common exceptions), prune plants once they have finished flowering.

- For coppicing, remove a third of the length of the stems every year. That way, every three years, you will have replaced the whole tree with fresh, new growth.

- Use sharp pruning shears or loppers and *always* clean them with disinfectant before you cut to prevent spreading diseases from plant to plant.

- Always cut just above a bud.

- Always cut the plant stem on the diagonal so that water does not sit on the wound.

CROP ROTATION

Crop rotation comes up time and again in gardening; in containers, of course, the problems you encounter in the ground are intensified unless you change the soil or compost every year.

Many of us grow vegetables in containers, but we also often grow the same species year after year, particularly if they were successful before. It is an age-old problem: we like a vegetable, but we don't have much space to grow it, so we buy a container or build a raised bed. With such a small amount of space, why would we want to grow things we don't like as much? However, crop rotation in edibles is essential, and this may mean growing a few crops that aren't on your initial wish list. I'm speaking from experience; I received lot of brassicas and, even though I had grown them the previous year, I just stuck them in my raised bed again. I could hardly harvest any of them. As the year progressed, cabbage root fly became more and more problematic, and aphids were rampant. Luckily, there was no clubroot in the soil, or I would have had to either wait twenty years or redo the entire bed. So, my advice is: it's not worth it. Grow different plants in each container every year, and you will have a much greater success rate.

Crop rotation is also great for biodiversity to mix things up. It keeps pests down, makes the crops perform better, prevents soil erosion, keeps weeds at bay, and has even been suggested to increase the amount of oxygen produced by plants.

In short, if you start right, plant right, feed right, water right, maintain your containers right, and don't always plant the same plants in the same places, then you should have containers that are not only beautiful but also functional and, importantly, that keep on giving year after year. Isn't it worth that little bit of thought and effort?

A simple rotation plan for optimal crop health:

LEAF
Brassicas (cabbage, kohlrabi, broccoli, sprouts, kale), chard, spinach, etc.

ROOT
Potatoes, parsnips, carrots, beets, radishes, turnips, celeriac, etc.

LEGUME
Beans, peas, fava beans, lima beans, lentils, etc.

FRUIT
Tomatoes, eggplant, pumpkins, peppers, etc. (can be substituted for grasses and *alliums* like corn, barley, onions, garlic, leeks, and chives)

INDEX

ACKNOWLEDGMENTS

This book was a collaborative effort in so many ways, and I am hugely indebted to the visionary people who created many of these beautiful containers. You all do a wonderful job, and I sincerely hope you keep doing it for many years to come. Thank you for giving us a glimpse.

First and foremost, I would like to thank Vicky Orchard and everybody at Kyle Books for giving me the opportunity to write this and turning my words into something I am hugely proud of. Second, to Rachel Warne, the most enormous thank you. Your photographs have brought this book to life and are more beautiful than I could have imagined. It was such a pleasure to work with you. Thank you also to Helen Bratby for the contemporary but beautifully tasteful design.

I would like to thank Ian Harris at Dawlish Gardens Trust. You have been a huge inspiration to me in my gardening work over the last few years, and if one day I have brought half the happiness to half as many people as you have, I will consider my time well spent. Thank you as well, and to Karen, for letting us take photos at DGT and giving me time off to write the book!

Thank you, Steve Briers. For everything. Your house made a stunning backdrop to the photographs, and a garden (and often a house) filled with potted plants isn't always easy to live with! So thank you for your support and patience.

A big thank you must also go to Steve Edney, once again, for your generosity in giving us free rein at The Salutation as well as to Louise Dowell for letting us invade your own garden. What a beautiful space.

Thank you to Fergus Garrett for allowing us to photograph the spectacular displays at Great Dixter. They were an inspiration.

I would also like to thank Ken White at Frosts Landscapes for the fantastic locations around London, as well as Colin Evans, for being such a great guide and ever so patient!

To Martin Woods (mwgardendesign. co.uk) for showing us and letting us photograph your beautiful garden (a must-see for anyone interested in containers!) Thank you also to Shelley Hugh-Jones. Your designs were stunning, and you were so helpful. Thank you to Claude Lester (vertigo. co.uk). Your potted roof terrace and green wall was fantastic. Thank you also to Francesca and Leandros at Langlea Garden Design. Also to Lahla Smart at Lahla Studios (lahlastudio. com) for the stunning magnetic pots. Thank you Mike Wateres at EZ Power steering UK (EZpowersteering.co.uk) for the visual feast of red and blue, and Tricia Kirkby at Garstone Garden Ornaments, Teignmouth, for letting us photograph one of my favorite living walls and the only historic car-trunk living wall I know of! A big thank you for your advice about bedding plants and for the photographs to MJ and LP Disney and Olde Barn Gardens holiday cottages, Dawlish. Thank you to Toby's reclamation in Exminster. I would like to say a special thank you to Chris Britton at High Garden Nurseries, Kenton, for the beautiful plants. I hope they enjoyed their holiday by the sea... Thank you also to Sophie de Bouvier at Branching Out Antiques, Wingham, Kent, and *Gardens Illustrated* and to The Original Hut company; The Hub, Bodiam, Kent, for letting us feature photos of your lovely containers.

Thank you, Dad, for lending me your beloved bonsai and driving us around the Kent and Sussex countryside in the rain. Thank you also to Bid and Mum for hunting out reclaimed containers (though I suspect you enjoyed it!).

Finally, a huge thank you to Libby (Olivia Rhodes), Michael Hibberd, Michael Punnet, Brian Mills, Holly Maries, and Laura Hunt for letting me invade your house and garden and build things—making a huge mess! You were all so welcoming and incredibly understanding.

Without all of your help, this book could not have happened, so thank you all so very much.